The KAMADO
Smoker & Grill
COOKBOOK

Delicious Recipes and Hands-on Techniques for
Mastering the World's Best Barbecue

Chris Grove

Ulysses Press

Published by
Ulysses Press
P.O. Box 3440
Berkeley, CA 94703
www.ulyssespress.com

ISBN: 978-1-61243-363-9
Library of Congress Catalog Number 2014932306

Printed in the United States by Bang Printing
13 12 11 10 9 8 7

Acquisitions editor: Katherine Furman
Managing editor: Claire Chun
Project editor: Alice Riegert
Editor: Phyllis Elving
Proofreader: Elyce Berrigan-Dunlop
Front cover design: what!design @ whatweb.com
Interior layout and design: what!design @ whatweb.com
Illustration page 3: © Suman Kasturia
Cover photograph: © Chris Grove
Interior photographs © Chris Grove except: page 32 (top left) © Jay Prince; page 60 (bottom left/right), page 208 © Brandi Shive; page 21, 29 (right), 37, 67, 119, 128 (left) © Alexis Grove
Food stylist: Alexis Grove
Index: Sayre Van Young

Distributed by Publishers Group West

IMPORTANT NOTE TO READERS: This book is independently authored and published and no sponsorship or endorsement of this book by, and no affiliation with, any trademarked brands of the kamado grill or other trademarked brands or products mentioned within is claimed or suggested. All trademarks that appear in this book belong to their respective owners and are used here for informational purposes only. The author and publisher encourage readers to patronize the quality brands and products mentioned in this book. Take special note of the important safety warnings on page 4, page 7, pages 199–202, and elsewhere throughout this book, and always use customary precautions for safe food preparation, handling, and storage.

CONTENTS

INTRODUCTION

I love green bell peppers, but my neighbor John doesn't like them. I only point that out because when I started thinking about what to include in this book, it made me want to offer something besides just a bunch of recipes to follow. People have specific taste preferences, and if a recipe includes something they don't like, they'll either not make it or leave that ingredient out — which could drastically change the result. So instead of only recipes, I want to provide kamado owners with inspiration and a toolkit of ideas to help them explore what their ceramic cookers can do. I want to give readers tips and techniques they might not have tried before. My sister bought her first kamado grill about a year ago and we have had countless emails, phone calls, and texts about discovering her new cooker. I want this book to capture the essence of all of those back-and-forth conversations so the information can be shared with anyone else who wants to learn the ins and outs of kamado grilling.

The tips and techniques that I share here aren't the only way to do things. I don't want to be "that guy" in barbecue forums who smugly berates someone because "you are doing it the wrong way." For example, ribs that are "fall off the bone" are generally acknowledged as overcooked in the barbecue community, especially in competitions. But if that's how you and your family like them, that's how you should cook them. If you prefer to foil your brisket and like the way it turns out, who cares if some guy in Texas says it isn't traditional?

Regardless of what I may lay out in this book, I hope that you will cook according to your own preferences and style.

I have often heard people mention that the kamado grill is a 3,000-year-old design. While the kamado, a wood-fired clay stove, has been in use in Japan for that long, the oval-shaped, self-contained grill is really a modern development.

The kamado's ceramics, airtight design, and vent controls make it much different than other grills. Kamados are extremely efficient with very little heat or moisture loss. You can run many kamados at 250°F for over 20 hours on one load of lump coal. The design also allows kamados to handle volatile, hot temperatures upwards of 700°F. The ceramic construction acts as a heat capacitor, storing heat and then releasing it steadily for stable cooking temperatures and evenly cooked food. When you are done cooking, the airtight design allows you to extinguish the coals and re-use the leftover coal the next time you cook.

CHOOSING YOUR KAMADO GRILL

You can't buy a better cooker for your home than a kamado-style grill. But this isn't a sales pitch, because I'm assuming that if you've bought this book, you already own a kamado.

In fact, I'm making a few assumptions based on my experiences with a lot of kamado owners. I suspect that you already have a basic understanding of grilling and maybe even smoking. If you're like a good majority of kamado grillers, you probably are intelligent, have a bit of a tech-geek side, stay up on but don't necessarily follow the latest trends, are open to ideas, and are a bit of a risk taker. Am I not too far off?

But on the off chance that you're just thumbing through, I'll offer a few pointers for buying a kamado grill. Kamados used to be limited to a few key brands, and you could only purchase them from authorized dealers. In the past few years, however, many new manufacturers have entered the game, and the number of places selling kamados has expanded rapidly. You can even buy them at big-box home improvement stores and warehouse clubs. And these aren't just poorly made knockoffs either. Most are quality kamados, and some include innovations that top the established brands. Here are some things to consider if you are buying a new kamado today.

Dealer or other retail outlet? With a dealer, you'll get a properly assembled kamado, delivery and setup (in most cases), and local assistance in case of warranty issues, but you will pay a premium. At other retail outlets you often get more accessories included and a significantly lower price, but you'll have to set up your kamado yourself and if things go wrong, you'll deal directly with the manufacturer. Both have their strong points, so it's a personal choice.

Heft and feel. A well-made kamado will feel solid when you open and close the dome lid (and vent controls). Open and close a few different models, and you'll quickly gain a sense of what feels like quality and what feels inferior. If it feels cheap (not the same as inexpensive), it probably is.

1. Top vent—also called dual-function metal top (DFMT), cast-iron vent, slide top

2. Dome thermometer

3. Dome lid

4. Side shelves—also called mates

5. Base

6. Bottom vent—also called draft door, slide vent

7. Cart—also called nest

8. Cooking grate—also called cooking grid, main grate

9. Fire ring—on some models, the fire ring and fire bowl may be combined as one piece.

10. Fire bowl—also called fire box

11. Fire grate—also called coal grate

KAMADO TERMINOLOGY

Different manufacturers have different terms for the various parts of their kamados, but the functions are mostly the same. For the purposes of this book, I'll be referring to the most common size of kamado, roughly 18½ inches in diameter.

Terms of warranty. A limited lifetime warranty on ceramics and a five-year warranty on metal parts are common, but you also have to consider how long the manufacturer has been in business.

Existing owners. The best information comes from those folks already using the specific brand. Check their user forums or go to a general barbecue forum like BBQ Brethren and search for comments on that brand. You will find a wealth of information— that is how I ended up buying my first kamado instead of the offset smoker trailer that I had my eye on.

READ THE MANUAL!

This book is in no way intended to replace or supersede your kamado owner's manual and manufacturer's recommendations. You should thoroughly read the manuals and check out the manufacturer's website for additional information. Most major manufacturers now have excellent online materials, including how-to videos and product-specific instructions.

FIRE MANAGEMENT

The single most important skill for success on any grill is mastering control of the fire. I wish it was as easy as saying that to get a kamado to 250°F, you simply open the bottom vent ¼ inch and have the top vent open ¼ inch.

Unfortunately, there are no universal settings for temperatures because conditions change, manufacturers' specifications vary, and there are just too many other variables.

We own two kamados of the same brand and size, and even they don't respond to the exact same settings. It would be like telling someone that to go 60 mph in a car, you hold your gas pedal 2.75 inches from the floorboard. You could be going uphill, downhill, or against the wind. You could have differing vehicle weights or tire pressures, and — well, you get the point. Your user manual will give some approximations for temperature settings, but these are just guidelines.

Just as with driving, it will take experience to master fire control. However, there are steps you can take to shorten the learning curve.

COAL SETUP IS THE KEY

Kamados function the best using quality lump coal, which is just pure wood that has been burned in an oxygen-poor environment. There are a lot of brands out there, but not all lump coal is created equal. Brands that use South American hardwoods are known for being "sparky," some to the point of leaving debris on your food. Some brands have mostly smaller pieces, which can clog air vents. Other brands have mostly large pieces that need to be broken up with a hammer for even lighting. Many brands, including some kamado manufacturer labels, are actually third party labels packaged by a single lump coal producer. The best way to find out about different brands is The Naked Whiz website's charcoal database (www.nakedwhiz.com/lumpindexpage.htm). Doug does a great job of giving impartial reviews using objective methods, keeping the reviews updated as brands change, and he also allows user reviews.

The best practice would be to remove and reserve any used coal from your kamado each time you use it. Clean out the ashes and make sure all vent holes on the inside are clear. In general, coal should be loaded to just above the air holes in the fire bowl, but **as** always, follow manufacturer instructions. When doing a long low-and-slow cook, I (and every kamado user I know) load the coal to at least the top of the fire bowl; some even cheat up into the fire ring. Load fresh lump at the bottom and top it off with the used coal that you've saved. This will give you the fastest starting and most trouble-free fire. If you have blocked air holes, your airflow will be restricted, and that will affect how well your temperature reacts to opening and closing the top and bottom vents.

Notice that I said "best practice." Honestly, if I'm doing a short cook at a medium-high temp, sometimes I'll cheat and just push the used coal to one side, adding new coal in the void. But for long-term or high-temp cooks, I clean it out first.

LIGHTING THE GRILL

You don't light a kamado the way you light most other grills. Sure, you can dump in a chimney full of lit coals, but you instantly lose the benefit of the kamado's tight air controls. Two specific lighting options are covered with the first two recipes in this book (on page 19 and page 23), but kamados are generally started by putting in unlit lump coal and using starter cubes, electric starters, or gas starters.

With a fresh load of lump coal in a clean kamado, you can reach grilling temperatures in as little as 15 minutes. With used coal and ash mixed in—if you fail to clean it out as mentioned above, it can take twice as long. Ironically, it takes longer to get the kamado smoking at 250°F than it does to start grilling at 350°F because you are waiting for the smoking wood to produce a clean smoke, which can take up to 45 minutes sometimes.

VENT POSITION

One thing that can help you get acclimated to using the bottom vent is to mark ½-inch increments on the slide vent, if not already done by the manufacturer, so you'll have a good idea how far it's open. It's more helpful to recognize that the vent is open one inch than to see that it's open "a little bit."

Some top vents are adjusted by screwing up or down, and those stay in place when you open the dome lid. But most use a sliding disc on a cap, and when you open the dome lid gravity is going to pull it downward, changing your setting. To avoid this, start at the pivot screw that holds the sliding disc and imagine a straight line going right across it. If you always rotate the cap so the imaginary line is aimed toward the back, as pictured below, it will stay in place when you open the lid.

COAST TO YOUR COOKING TEMPERATURE

Stopping the temperature at your desired cooking temperature is much like docking a boat—you have to start slowing down before you get there. For example, if my target is 350°F, I might close the bottom vent from wide open to about halfway shut when the temperature reaches 275°F. Then as it hits 300°F, I'll close it a little more. If

the temperature is still rising when it hits 325°F, I might close it down even farther so that I coast up to 350°F. If you're coming to a kamado from other grills, you will quickly

notice that your vents are significantly more effective at controlling the temperature with this grill.

DON'T FLIP YOUR LID

Kamados are designed to be used with the dome lid closed, and it should be kept closed as much as possible while in use. The tight tolerances and high efficiency of the kamado depend on it being operated as a closed system with the airflow closely controlled by the lower and top vents. For all recipes in this book, presume that all cooking is done with the dome lid closed unless I explicitly instruct to leave the lid open. Cooking with the dome lid shut is the default mode when using a kamado because that closed system is what regulates temperatures.

Every time the dome lid opens, the vents are pointless and the coals get unlimited access to air, causing the temperature to

FIRE SAFETY

What's a flashback? Good question, let's talk fire safety for a minute. Once again, you should read and heed your manufacturer's user manual and all safety instructions.

A flashback is a quick way to remove your eyebrows, or worse. This is a phenomenon specific to kamados because of their tight air controls—but it isn't a design fault, rather a condition caused by fire management. You just don't notice it in most other types of grills because they have so many air leaks that flashback conditions are less likely to occur.

To have a fire, you need the "fire triangle"—heat, oxygen, and fuel. If you have a hot fire in the kamado and suddenly cut down the airflow by closing the bottom vent, you've created a fire that is starving for oxygen. When the dome lid opens, air rushes in and the superheated gases (volatile organic compounds) suddenly ignite in a fireball that jumps up and out of the kamado—right to where you are standing. It can cause serious burns and is no joke.

The way to avoid a flashback is to re-introduce air slowly. Crack the lid open just an inch a few times in rapid succession before you open it all the way. Train yourself to do this every time you open your kamado.

This is also one more reason that you should always wear personal protective equipment (PPE), such as safety glasses and long-sleeved heat-resistant gloves. When it comes to gloves, there are a lot of options out there, but you have to be careful in choosing. Silicone oven mitts are quite the rage *in the kitchen* because they are comfortable, handle "high heat," and come in cute shapes that look like pig or cow puppets. But your kamado can generate much higher temperatures than most home ovens. The hot ceramics of a heat deflector can melt or burn through many kitchen oven mitts in seconds. Heavy-duty leather welding gloves work better for grilling duty. Even with these brutes, you have to handle hot ceramics very quickly and have a "landing spot" already cleared and waiting.

Are you "screening your coals"? Lump coal is a natural wood product that often will pop at high temperatures. Sometimes this sends a hot cinder shooting out of the bottom vent. If your kamado bottom vent has a secondary slide screen, keep it closed to contain those cinders.

That brings up another couple of points. Don't leave a burning grill unattended. Using a grill mat under your grill to minimize damage from errant coals is especially recommended if you are grilling on a wooden deck. Don't skimp on a cheaper gas grill mat. Those are much less expensive, but they are only meant to resist greasy drippings and aren't fire resistant.

rise. But what can you do when you use a technique that requires frequent opening for food handling, such as cooking on a wok or griddle? First, in such cases I'll start off a little lower than my intended temperature because I know it will rise during the cook. Second, I'll have everything I need before I open the lid, and I'll work quickly. Third, I'll shut the lower vent to about ½ inch after I shut the dome lid, to settle down the fire. You do have to be careful with the third step because this can set up a flashback.

MAINTENANCE

Any grill requires cleaning and maintenance to perform at its peak, and the kamado is no exception. You should follow the specific maintenance recommendations in your user's manual, but here are some general guidelines.

EVERY TIME

Each time you use your kamado, clean out the ashes from the prior use and make sure the internal air holes are clear. I keep a lidded metal bucket and dustpan near our kamados for this purpose. Small coals can remain alive for hours insulated in the ash, so never dump ashes straight into a trash can.

QUARTERLY

Even if you do the light clean-out every time you use your kamado, some ash will fall through the fire box air holes and end up between the fire box and kamado base. Unless you have spaghetti noodles for arms, you won't be able to reach around to these spots through the bottom vent. Over repeated use, these little bits will build up into piles big enough to block airflow around the fire box.

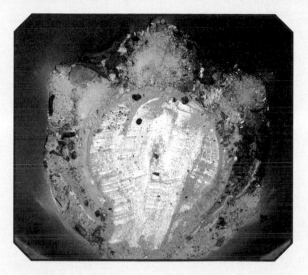

To clear the debris, you have to remove the interior ceramics and sweep out the kamado base. Some people get around this by using a shop vac rigged with a piece of flexible rubber hose that fits through the vent and around the back. Only do this if your grill hasn't been used for several days, because of the threat of live embers lurking in the ash.

HIGH-TEMP CLEAN BURN

Over time, buildup will occur on the inside of your kamado. This happens faster with low-and-slow cooks than it does if you're mostly just grilling. But eventually it will build up, impairing the ceramic's ability to reflect heat. You can clean off this buildup by using a high-temp clean burn. Here's one way to do that.

1 Remove the internal ceramics. Use a wire brush or a ball of crushed aluminum foil to scrub the interior walls. Don't worry about getting everything — this is just a "pre-scrub."

2 Replace the internal ceramics and fill the fire box with coal. Open the bottom and top vents all of the way, light a fire, shut the dome lid, and let it burn until it runs out of coal. This will take just a couple of hours at the extreme temperatures, and the ceramics will get quite hot. Let the kamado cool overnight.

3 Once cooled, remove the internal ceramics again and repeat the brushing. This time, all the crud should come off easily as black dust that can just be swept out.

4 Put everything back together and you're done.

Finally, routinely check the tightness of the bolts that tighten the metal bands that hold the exterior ceramics in place. These can loosen over time and often after high-temp clean burns. If you let them get too loose, the dome lid could actually fall off when you open it.

Don't Blow a Gasket, Man!

The gasket or seal between the dome lid and base is the Achilles' heel of the kamado. Manufacturers recommend cooking at lower temperatures for the first few times to cure the adhesives. It's so common to damage the gasket at high temps that I consider it more of a consumable supply than a part. You are most likely to torch a gasket in two situations. One is when the dome and base aren't properly aligned, so that some of the seal is directly exposed to heat. The other is a high-temp cook with the heat deflector in "legs down" position, because this directs hot gases outward right at the level of the seal.

The good news is, you *really* don't *need* a gasket. I ran a kamado with no gasket for almost four years without any ill effects, even on long low-and-slow cooks. So one option is to not replace the gasket if you toast it by accident.

Another option is replacing the torched gasket with a high-temperature gasket made from fire-resistant Nomex. Removing the old gasket can be difficult using hand tools, but a 3M paint and rust stripper pad on a drill will make quick work of it without damaging the ceramics.

Yet a third option that a lot of kamado owners have used is replacing the gasket with a wood stove rope-style gasket. It should be noted that the makers of these gaskets haven't approved them for food handling, so read about the potential risks before going this route. We replaced one of ours with such a gasket, and it has survived more than 100 cooks without incident.

Accessorizing Is Everything!

There seem to be an infinite number of grilling accessories, many specifically for kamados. As a grilling blogger, I have an inbox full of the latest offerings. Some are innovative and impressive, while the majority are just toys or gimmicks. Here are some of the more useful grilling accessories, in my opinion.

Must-Have Accessories

Instant-read thermometer. This is the only way to truly know if your food is properly cooked. You want a high-quality thermometer that's truly instant-read—meaning three seconds or less. If you're grilling six steaks and use a slow thermometer, the time it takes to check all six steaks is enough to go from medium-rare to medium. The gold standard among serious grillers is the Thermapen by Thermoworks.

Remote probe thermometer. This thermometer's wired probe lets you continuously monitor internal temps while food is cooking. This is essential for smoking, roasting, and reverse searing. Upper-end models include options such as dual probes (to measure cooking and internal temps at the same time), wireless capability, and some data logging.

Heat deflector setup. This is needed for most indirect setups on the kamado. Most kamado brands include the deflector as part of the package, but not all do. If yours doesn't come with a deflector, you will definitely need to buy one.

Leather welding gloves. Found at home improvement stores, these are long-sleeved and heavy-duty. They work better than any oven mitts that I've tried and usually are just as cheap.

Quality wire brush. Loose brass bristles can get on food and cause serious intestinal injuries. Cheap brushes often have short lengths of wire stuck into holes, making it easy for them to fall out. Quality brushes fold longer lengths of wire and pin them down in the brush, making them less likely to be dislodged.

Wiggle rod. This is just a wire rod with a bent tip, used for clearing any blocked holes that develop during a cook. Just take a metal skewer and bend 1 inch of the tip at a 90° angle. Slide it through the bottom vent, stick it up through the fire grate holes, and wiggle it to dislodge any ash or small pieces of coal blocking the airflow.

Pizza stone. Some models made for home kitchens are too thin to handle the heat of a kamado, so spend the extra money to get a thick, grill-safe pizza stone.

Raised cooking grid. These are very useful for adding capacity and for cooking "raised direct" (page 114). Manufacturers offer different styles, or you can easily build your own as described on page 114.

Long-handled tongs. Kamados generate some serious heat, and you don't want to be burning your knuckles while turning 30 chicken wings with six-inch serving tongs.

Drip pan. This will keep your heat deflector clean and avoid a greasy fire. Foil pans work, but you can't beat a 13-inch, foil-covered deep-dish pizza pan.

Accessories That Are Nice to Have

Cast-iron grates. I had a hard time not putting this into the "must have" category, but there are plenty of people who have great success just using standard stock grates. Cast-iron grates have excellent heat conductivity and sear gorgeous crosshatch marks. I use them for almost every cook, even when I'm not searing, because I think they help with even heating and are easier to maintain when used frequently. The down side is that if you don't use them often, they can rust quickly if they're left out or get damp where stored.

Aftermarket fire grates. A few companies are offering fire grates that use different configurations than the standard holes in a cast-iron disc, which gets clogged. High-Que makes one with stainless-steel bars, and the Saint Louis Charcoal Company offers one made of expanded stainless steel. These aftermarket fire grates replace the stock grate and greatly eliminate fire management issues caused by clogged air holes.

Table. While the standard carts and shelves provide some working space, I greatly prefer the stability and work area that a kamado table provides. Plus, if you buy an unfinished stock table from a supplier, you can add your own custom touches, such as a tile top and varnish or stain.

Stoneware. Stoneware pans, pie plates, and loaf pans will help you get the most out of your kamado as an oven. While metal pans can be used, I find that stoneware's heat conductivity provides more even cooking.

Electronic controllers. These devices can regulate a kamado with a PID controller that reads the cooking temperature and turns a fan mounted on your bottom vent on and off as needed. Read more about electronic controllers on page 146.

Lighting system. A gas torch (page 23) or an electronic starter is the easiest and quickest to fire up your kamado.

Wok. The kamado is the perfect setup for stir-firing (page 91). A wok will help you incorporate quick, healthy meals into your grilling routine.

Temperatures for Cooking Meat

	Rare	Medium Rare	Medium	Medium Well	Well	USDA Minimum (as of 6/15/13)
Beef, Veal, and Lamb						
Steaks & Chops	125–130°F	130–135°F	135–140°F	150°F	160°F	145°F with 3 minute rest
Approximate Cooking Times for 1-inch Steak at 450°F	3 minutes per side	4 minutes per side	4–5 minutes per side	5–6 minutes per side	7 minutes per side	5 minutes per side
Whole Roasts	125–130°F	130–135°F	135–140°F	150°F	160°F	145°F with 3 minutes rest
Ground Meat						160°F
Brisket					195–205°F "like butter" test	
Pork						
Chops			145°F		160°F	145°F
Roasts (Loins, Tenderloins)			145°F		160°F	145°F
Ham (Fresh, Raw)			145°F			145°F
Ham (Cooked)			140°F			145°F
Butts, Shoulders					195–200°F	
Ground						160°F
Poultry						
White Meat					160°F	165°F
Dark Meat					175–180°F	165°F
Ground					165°F	165°F
Fish						
Dense Flesh like Tuna, Salmon			120°F		145°F	
Other Fish			140°F		145°F	

Rack/pan combo. If you ever plan on doing roasts on your kamado—and you should—you'll want some type of roasting rack and a pan to fit under it.

Grill pan/veggie wok. These are typically some type of metal pan with small holes that allow for quick cooking of loose vegetables on the grill top.

GrillGrates. These go on top of your normal cooking grate (page 121). They prevent flare-ups (which shouldn't be a problem on a kamado) and channel the heat through raised ribs that give supercharged sear marks. If you like to show off well-defined grill marks, these are for you.

KAMADO CULTURE

Kamado owners are a unique bunch and are extremely willing to share their ideas. I would highly recommend that you get involved in an online kamado forum, at least while you learn to master your grill. Most manufacturers operate a forum, some more active than others. Other forums are not brand specific. Find one that you are comfortable with and at least lurk, reading what other kamado users are up to.

Some brands have festivals at which users get together regionally once a year to celebrate the kamado. Festival-goers grill recipes for sampling, exchange techniques, tell tall tales, and have an adult beverage or two. These are good fun and definitely worth the trip.

BASIC RECIPES

These are recipes that I developed while writing my grilling and BBQ blog, Nibble Me This, over the past few years. They are staples that I use frequently at home and throughout this book.

NMT BASIC BBQ RUB

This simple, all-purpose BBQ rub is good with both chicken and pork. I like to use oregano and thyme leaves for my dried herbs.

Makes 1½ cups

½ cup smoked paprika

¼ cup packed dark brown sugar

¼ cup turbinado sugar

¼ cup kosher salt

5 tablespoons garlic pepper seasoning

2 teaspoons dried herbs of your choice

2 teaspoons chili powder

1 teaspoon chipotle chile powder

1 Mix all the ingredients together and store in an airtight container. Grind for finer texture right before using.

NMT Cajun Beef Rub

This is the mix I use when I want a beef rub that has the flavors of the Bayou.

Makes about ¼ cup

2 tablespoons smoked paprika

2 teaspoons kosher salt

2 teaspoons onion powder

2 teaspoons garlic powder

1 teaspoon cayenne

1 teaspoon red pepper flakes

1½ teaspoons white pepper

½ teaspoon black pepper

1 teaspoon dried thyme

1 teaspoon oregano

IIIIIIIIIIIIIIIIIIIIIIIIIIIIIIIIIIIIIIIIIIIIIIIIIIIIIIIIIIIIII

1 Mix all the ingredients together and store in an airtight container until ready to use, for up to 6 months.

NMT Beef Rub

When I'm cooking beef steaks, roasts, or brisket, this is the rub that I often use. It's best when stored with the coarse bits intact, then freshly ground to use as needed. I use Bourbon Barrel Smoke Sea Salt, and I get my dried bell peppers from Penzeys Spices (3/8-inch-cut flakes).

Makes about 1¼ cups

5 tablespoons coarse smoked salt

2 tablespoons black peppercorns

1 tablespoon green peppercorns

1 tablespoon dried minced garlic

1 tablespoon dried red and green bell pepper flakes

2¼ teaspoons dried minced onion

2 teaspoons dried thyme leaves

IIIIIIIIIIIIIIIIIIIIIIIIIIIIIIIIIIIIIIIIIIIIIIIIIIIIIIIIIIIIII

1 Mix all the ingredients together and store in an airtight container. Grind to a finer texture just before using the rub.

NMT Burger Mix-in

Many commercially available burger seasonings look like they have thrown the entire spice cabinet into a jar. I like this one because it is so simple, providing the classic burger flavor without over seasoning it.

Makes about ½ cup

¼ cup kosher salt

2 tablespoons ground black pepper

1 tablespoon dried minced garlic

1 tablespoon dried minced onion

||||||||||||||||||||||||||||||||||||||||||||||||||||||

I   Mix all the ingredients together and store in an airtight container. To use, mix in 1½ teaspoons per pound of ground beef.

NMT Blackening Seasoning

Just adding this seasoning to a protein does not make it "blackened." Season it with this rub and then cook on a fiery hot cast iron, while drizzling the meat with butter.

Makes 2 tablespoons

½ tablespoon paprika

1¼ teaspoons kosher salt

½ teaspoon onion powder

½ teaspoon garlic powder

½ teaspoon cayenne pepper

½ teaspoon black pepper

½ teaspoon white pepper

¼ teaspoon thyme, ground

¼ teaspoon oregano, ground

¼ teaspoon celery seed

||||||||||||||||||||||||||||||||||||||||||||||||||||||||||||||

I   Mix all of the ingredients together and store in an airtight container for up to 6 months.

NMT Spicy Poultry Rub

This spicy poultry rub is good for grilling chicken with a bit of a kick to use in sandwiches, tacos, or wraps.

Makes ¼ cup

2 tablespoons seasoned salt

2 teaspoons turbinado sugar

2 teaspoons smoked paprika

1 teaspoon ancho chile powder

1 teaspoon chili powder

1 teaspoon ground black pepper

1 teaspoon garlic powder

1 teaspoon dried oregano

1 teaspoon dried orange peel

||||||||||||||||||||||||||||||||||||||||||||||||||||||||

1   Mix all the ingredients together and store in an airtight container.

NMT Cherry BBQ Sauce

This sweet and spicy sauce goes well with both chicken and pork.

Makes about 2 cups

⅓ cup ketchup

¼ cup Sweet Baby Ray's Barbecue Sauce

½ cup cherry preserves

¼ cup cherry juice

¼ cup packed dark brown sugar

3 tablespoons apple cider vinegar

1½ tablespoons chipotle hot sauce

½ tablespoon Worcestershire sauce

½ teaspoon dried minced garlic

½ teaspoon dried onion flakes

¼ teaspoon ground black pepper

¼ teaspoon ground cumin, preferably roasted ground cumin

⅛ teaspoon ground coriander

⅛ teaspoon liquid smoke

2 or 3 pinches chipotle chile powder

Smoked salt to taste (about ½ teaspoon)

||||||||||||||||||||||||||||||||||||||||||||||||||||||||

1   Mix all the ingredients together in a saucepan on the stovetop. Bring to a simmer over medium heat and let simmer for 5 minutes, stirring occasionally. Blend to a smooth consistency using an immersion blender. Let cool, place in an airtight container, and store in the refrigerator for up to one month.

NMT Basic Brine

This brine will help flavor and add moisture to your poultry and pork. For a quick brine — less than 4 hours — you can increase the salt to ½ cup.

Makes 2 quarts

2 quarts distilled water

¼ cup kosher salt

¼ cup sugar

1 tablespoon dried minced garlic

1 teaspoon red pepper flakes

|||||||||||||||||||||||||||||||||||||||||||||||

I   Stir all the ingredients together until the salt and sugar have dissolved.

Lisbon-Style Vinegar BBQ Sauce

Fashioned after a recipe given to me by my grandmother, this is similar to the sauce used by the fire department in her small farming community to make smoked pork shoulders for their annual fundraiser. This is a Piedmont-style sauce, spicy and tangy. I drizzle it very lightly over my smoked pork as a final seasoning before serving.

Makes a little over 1 cup

1 cup apple cider vinegar

3 tablespoons sugar

1 tablespoon kosher salt

1 tablespoon ketchup

1 tablespoon squeezable buttery spread

1 tablespoon honey

½ teaspoon ground black pepper

½ teaspoon red pepper flakes

||||||||||||||||||||||||||||||||||||||||||||||||||||||||||

I   Mix all the ingredients together in a small saucepan on the stovetop. Bring to a simmer over medium heat, stirring to combine thoroughly. Let cool, cover, and store in the refrigerator.

#1

PAPER TOWEL LIGHTING METHOD

Many kamado manufacturers suggest lighting the grill with either paraffin wax starter cubes or an electric starter. But most people I know or encounter in BBQ forums use one of these alternative techniques instead: the paper towel method shown here or the torch method described on page 23. Regardless of how you prefer to light your kamado, you should be familiar with the paper towel method, because it comes in handy when you're out of starter cubes or gas, or your electric starter is on the fritz.

The procedure is straightforward:

1. Load your coal as instructed by the manufacturer.

2. Lightly drizzle cooking oil in a zig-zag pattern on a standard paper towel. Tightly roll up the towel to form a long wick.

3   Place the towel on top of the coal and overlap some coal on top of it — but don't bury it.

4   Light both ends of the towel.

5   Close the kamado and open the bottom and top vents all the way.

In 15 minutes, your grill should start coming up to temperature. Start adjusting the vents to a more closed position as you approach your desired cooking temperature.

The beauty of this trick is that it works every time, and you almost always have paper towels and oil without having to make a special trip. So even if you already light your kamado grill a different way, try using this method to fire up your grill. While you're at it, grill up these moist and tasty pork chops!

Spinach-Stuffed Pork Chops

Serves: 4   Prep Time: 20 minutes   Grill Time: 20 minutes

4 bone-in rib pork chops, 1 inch thick

For the Stuffing
1 tablespoon unsalted butter

2 tablespoons pine nuts

4 cups lightly packed fresh baby spinach

4 ounces Neufchâtel or cream cheese

¼ teaspoon cayenne pepper

¼ teaspoon kosher salt, or to taste

For the Dry Rub
1 teaspoon kosher salt

1 teaspoon ground black pepper

1 teaspoon smoked paprika

½ teaspoon turbinado sugar or light brown sugar

½ teaspoon granulated garlic

1   To make the stuffing, melt the butter on the stovetop in a saucepan over medium heat. Toast the pine nuts in the butter until golden brown and fragrant, about 2 to 3 minutes. Remove the pine nuts from the pan and chop; set aside.

2   Place the spinach in the pan with the butter until it wilts down, about 4 to 5 minutes. Remove, drain well, and chop.

3   In a bowl, mix together the Neufchâtel or cream cheese, wilted spinach, toasted pine nuts, cayenne, and ¼ teaspoon salt. Taste for seasoning and add more salt if desired. (You can make the stuffing up to 12 hours ahead of time. Cover and refrigerate until ready to use.)

4   Set up your kamado for direct heat (page 27). Try out the paper towel method to light it. Preheat the grill to 400°F–425°F.

5   Mix the rub ingredients together in a small bowl. Use a sharp knife to cut a pocket into the side of each pork chop.

Season the pork chops inside and out with the rub mixture.

6 Stuff each pork chop with some of the spinach/cheese mixture and close the pocket with toothpicks. (Note how many toothpicks you use to seal the chops. You want to make sure you remove them all before serving!)

7 With the lid down, grill the chops for 4 minutes per side.

Then turn them onto the rib bone end so they are "standing" upright.

This will keep the cheese mixture from leaking out as it heats. Cook until the internal temperature reaches 140°F, about 5 minutes longer. Measure the temperature by inserting the thermometer in the solid meat at the back of the pocket, not in the middle of the cheese mixture.

8 Remove the pork chops from the grill and serve.

#2

GAS TORCH LIGHTING METHOD

What can you do with the power of 3,600°F in your hands? Besides soldering and brazing copper tubes, you can start your kamado with it!

Gas torches are a popular choice for lighting because they are one of the fastest ways to get your coal glowing red. And let's face it — torches are cool. The two types normally used are MAP-Pro (yellow) or a weed burner attachment for a propane

tank. You can buy either at most tool stores or many home improvement stores. Don't use a handheld propane (blue) torch, as it will sputter out when held upside down.

Torches are no joke, and you should read the manufacturer's directions carefully. When the intense heat of the flame hits coal, the coal will often pop with a loud crack and shoot off black cinders. Follow the safety guidelines from the supplier and wear safety glasses and heat-resistant gloves when using a torch.

The procedure is quick:

I   Open the bottom and top vents all the way.

2   Open your kamado and light three different coal areas for 20 seconds each. These should be spaced evenly — I light the coals at 10, 2, and 6 o'clock.

3   Shut the grill. In about 10 minutes your kamado will start to come up to temperature.

Since we're standing around using torches, let's make some burgers. I really like the jalapeño white Cheddar cheese on this burger, but you can use pepper jack cheese if you can't find the Cheddar. You can make the chili in advance and then reheat it before serving, adding a tablespoon or so of beef stock.

Game Day Chili Cheeseburger

Serves: 4   Prep Time: 1 hour for making the chili (can be made ahead) and 40 minutes for the burgers   Grill Time: 8 to 10 minutes

1½ pounds ground round

2¼ teaspoons NMT Burger Mix-in (page 16)

4 Kaiser rolls

Olive oil or melted butter, for brushing the rolls

4 slices jalapeño white Cheddar cheese

8 slices cooked bacon

½ cup diced Vidalia onion

For the Chili Sauce

1¼ pounds ground round

½ cup beef stock

¼ cup picante sauce or salsa

3 tablespoons ketchup

⅓ teaspoon celery salt

⅓ teaspoon ground black pepper

1½ teaspoons dark brown sugar

2 teaspoons chili powder

1 teaspoon ground cumin

½ teaspoon dried minced onion

¼ teaspoon ground coriander

½ teaspoon white vinegar

½ teaspoon seasoned salt, or to taste

I   For the chili sauce, mix all the chili ingredients together in a medium saucepan and heat on a stovetop over medium-high heat. I know it seems weird not to brown the ground beef first but once I tried it this way, I switched to it. Break the beef up as it cooks in the sauce. Bring to a boil, then reduce the heat and simmer, stirring occasionally, until the chili reduces to a thick saucelike consistency, about 45 minutes to 1 hour. Taste for seasoning and add more salt if desired.

2   To make the burger patties, rinse your hands with cold water and use them to mix the ground round and NMT Burger Mix-in together. Divide into 4 equal portions and form into 5-inch patties. Refrigerate for 30 minutes.

3   Set up your kamado grill for direct heat (page 27) and start your fire. Preheat the grill to 450°F.

4   Slice the Kaiser rolls in half. Lightly brush the insides with a little olive oil or melted butter. Place on the grill cut side down until toasted, about 15 seconds. Remove and set aside.

5 Grill the burger patties for 3½ minutes per side.

6 Build your burgers by topping the bottom half of each roll with a beef patty, 2 strips of bacon, some chili sauce, and onions. Add the bun tops and serve.

Top with the cheese slices during the last minute.

#3

DIRECT GRILLING

Direct grilling is what most people visualize when they think of grilling—burgers, steaks, or chops on a grate over a bed of fiery red coals. And that's pretty much it, although there are a couple of differences to be aware of with a kamado compared to a standard kettle-style grill.

The first is that kamado grills are deeper and have steeper sides. This makes it a little difficult to set up and manage the "two-zone fire" that some general grilling recipes call for, unless you use additional equipment and techniques. We'll get into that with indirect grilling (page 31), sear/roasting (page 75), and reverse searing (page 78). A two- or three-zone fire is possible in larger kamados or oblong ones with a firebox divider, such as the Primo Oval. It's just not ideal in most average-size kamados.

The second thing to know is that dome temperatures are only half the story. The distance between the coals and the food plays a big part. Here's an experiment I ran to demonstrate this point. I loaded one kamado full of coal and a second kamado only half full. I preheated both to 350°F according to the calibrated dome thermometers. I placed a quarter sheet pan in each for five minutes and then measured the pan temperature in several locations, using a non-contact laser thermometer.

Despite identical dome temperatures, the pan temperatures averaged 24.6°F higher in the full kamado than in the half-full one. Also, the full kamado's pan temperatures were more consistent from spot to spot, while they varied by up to 60°F in the half-full kamado. There were four inches between pan and coal in the full kamado, compared to seven or eight inches in the half-full grill.

While both had air temperatures of 350°F, the pan in the loaded kamado received significantly more infrared energy. If it had been a steak instead of a pan, it would have cooked faster in the full grill. (For an excellent summary of energy and cooking, go to amazingribs.com/tips_and_technique/thermodynamics_of_cooking.html.)

All of that is just to say that it's important to fill your coal to the same level every time when grilling direct. That will keep you from wondering why it turned out perfectly last time when you grilled for ten minutes at 350°F but wasn't finished this time after the same ten minutes at 350°F.

Other than that, the direct grilling setup is just a cooking grate placed on top of the fire ring.

These steaks are just the ticket for practicing a direct cook. The Cajun butter makes twice what you need for the steaks so that you can use it to help rock out some potatoes, too.

GRILLED STRIP STEAKS WITH CAJUN BUTTER

Serves: 4   Prep Time: 15 minutes if you make the butter ahead of time   Grill Time: 10 minutes

4 strip steaks, 1 inch thick
8 teaspoons finely ground NMT Beef Rub
(page 15)

FOR THE CAJUN BUTTER
½ cup (1 stick) unsalted butter, softened
¼ teaspoon granulated garlic

¼ teaspoon celery salt
¼ teaspoon dried thyme leaves
¼ teaspoon red pepper flakes
⅛ teaspoon ground white pepper
⅛ teaspoon onion powder
⅛ teaspoon ground black pepper

1   To make the Cajun butter, work the dry ingredients into the butter in a small bowl; mix thoroughly. Divide into 8 portions, place on wax paper, and refrigerate for 30 minutes before serving.

2   Set up your kamado for direct heat and preheat it to 500°F.

3   Season the steaks on all sides with the beef rub.

4   Grill the steaks with the lid closed until they reach an internal temperature of 127°F for medium-rare, about 4 minutes per side (see Temperatures for Cooking Meat on page 13). For the classic

crosshatch marks, rotate the steaks a quarter turn while grilling each side.

5 Remove the steaks from the grill and immediately top each with a portion of the Cajun butter. Let rest for 5 minutes and then serve.

#4
INDIRECT GRILLING

The techniques for indirect grilling are markedly different on a kamado than on a standard kettle grill or most gas grills. This can present a learning curve for people switching to a kamado for the first time.

With a kettle grill, you bank the coals to one side, put the food on the other side, and cover it with a lid for indirect cooking. In a gas grill you turn a burner on at one end and cook on the other end with the lid closed. But if you try to put coals to one side of a kamado, they will all end up at the bottom center because of the steep walls, and you will still pretty much be cooking directly over the heat.

Instead, the most common way to set up a kamado for indirect grilling is to use a heat deflector that blocks most of the direct heat but allows convective heat into the cooking area. The names and styles of these deflectors vary among manufacturers, but most utilize a ceramic disc (like a pizza stone) supported on the fire ring by some type of structure, as pictured.

This allows you to set a drip pan on the deflector to keep it clean. My favorite general-purpose drip pan is a 13½-inch deep-dish pizza pan that I picked up at a restaurant supply store years ago for about $8.

When cooking indirectly, it is preferable to preheat the grill to your cooking temperature, or at least close to it, before putting the indirect setup into the kamado. This seems faster to me than setting up for indirect heat and then preheating.

For most indirect cooking, I place the heat deflector on the fire ring with the legs up. The legs hold the cooking grate about three to four inches above the deflector.

It covers almost the entire deflector, compared to square foil pans that leave areas exposed. I cover the pan with foil so I never have to clean it, because I'm lazy like that.

Always be aware of where your hot spots are for indirect cooking.

Anywhere directly above the gaps will be hotter, because that's where the heat gets into the cooking area from below. At lower temperatures, as for smoking (page 40), the temperature differences aren't that big a deal. But when you're cooking at high temperatures, as for roasting (page 55), these hot spots can be drastic and will burn food left there for long.

Meat loaf sometimes gets a bad rap. I blame that on sitcoms needing an easy joke: "So-and-so's cooking is sooooo bad...." But in kamado and online barbecue forums, meat loaf is actually quite popular, and for good reason. Fire-roasted meat loaf is slightly smoky, tangy, and delectable! Do you know what's even better than meat loaf from the kamado? A meat loaf sandwich at 3 in the morning while the rest of the family is snoozing in their beds.

For the smoked sausage in this recipe, I use a fresh smoked cook-and-serve type sausage (like the Conecuh brand) instead of fully cooked or ready-to-eat sausage. I use an off-the-shelf Southwest seasoning blend, but you can use your own mixture if you have a favorite recipe. If you really like your meat loaf smoky, you can add wood chips to the coal, but I find that it gets enough smoke from the burning lump coal.

Fire-Roasted Meat Loaf Sandwiches

Serves: 8   Prep Time: 1 hour, including rest time   Grill Time: 1 to 1½ hours

1 pound ground round

1 pound ground pork

¼ pound fresh smoked pork sausage (uncooked)

Sourdough bread

Sandwich makings such as lettuce, onion, tomato slices, and cheese

For the Dry Mix

1 cup panko bread crumbs

2 teaspoons Southwest seasoning

1 teaspoon ground black pepper

1½ teaspoons dried minced garlic

1 tablespoon dried oregano

For the Wet Mix

4 egg yolks

½ teaspoon hot sauce

1½ teaspoons Worcestershire sauce

1½ teaspoons spicy brown mustard

1½ teaspoons horseradish sauce

½ cup diced onion

½ cup diced red bell pepper

For the Glaze

½ cup ketchup

¼ cup packed dark brown sugar

1 tablespoon apple cider vinegar

1 teaspoon hot sauce

1   Fold the ground round, ground pork, and sausage together in a large bowl.

2   Mix the dry mix ingredients together in a small bowl and fold into the meat mixture.

3   Stir the wet mix ingredients together and fold into the meat mixture.

4   Form the mixture into a loaf and let rest for 30 minutes in the refrigerator to firm. I don't use a loaf pan, because that holds the grease in while the meat loaf cooks. If you have a wire loaf pan, use that. Otherwise, simply support the meat loaf on aluminum foil, a mesh pizza screen, or a "Frogmat," which is a mesh grill topper sold online and at grill stores.

5   Preheat your kamado to 350°F and set it up for indirect heat.

6   Place the meat loaf on the grill grate above the drip pan, close the lid, and cook for 45 minutes.

7   Whisk together the glaze ingredients in a small saucepan on the stovetop over low heat. Brush the glaze onto the top and sides of the loaf, close the lid, and

cook until the meat reaches an internal temperature of 165°F. Total cooking time will be about 1¼ to 1½ hours. Remove from the grill and let rest for 5 minutes.

8 Slice and serve. For the record, optimal serving includes slices of Mary Alice's Sourdough Bread (page 163), lettuce, red onion, tomato, and cheese—at 3 o'clock in the morning.

TRY THIS NEXT!
Use the indirect heat technique to give your favorite baked ziti recipe a spin on your kamado.

#5
SPATCHCOCKED POULTRY

Spatchcocked chicken is perhaps the most popular way to cook whole poultry on a kamado grill. Splitting and flattening a chicken promotes fast and even cooking regardless of whether you are grilling, roasting, or smoking it. (It works great for roasting chickens in the oven, too, but why would you want to do that?)

If you have a full-service butcher, you could just buy a bird already spatchcocked, but it's easy enough to do yourself with a pair of poultry sheers or a good sharp knife. Place the bird on a cutting board, breast side down. Using the sheers or knife, carefully cut down one side of the backbone.

For grilling, the popular technique is to use the raised direct method (page 114) and cook the chicken at 375°F, skin side up, for one hour—no flipping required. Quick, easy, and better than any grocery store rotisserie chicken, this is what I do most often. Any flavor profile works for this, including standards such as lemon pepper, barbecue seasoning, or a mixture of herbs.

Repeat on the other side and remove the backbone. Some folks remove the sternum or keel bone at this point, but I don't bother. Instead, I just flip the bird over, breast side up. Put the heel of your hand on the center of the breast and give it a quick, forceful, CPR-style push downwards, cracking the bones in the breast.

For smoking a spatchcocked bird, as in the following recipe, it's a good idea to brine it first to ensure that it stays juicy during the long cook. It's important to thoroughly dry the poultry after brining, or the skin won't get crispy. If you have time, even let it air-dry in the fridge for a few hours.

Hickory is my choice for poultry, but you can use whatever smoking woods you like. Poultry can absorb excess smoke, but I haven't run into that problem on a kamado as long as I have a clean-burning fire to start with. Smoke the poultry with the skin side up. Mopping a sauce on during the cook will add layers of seasoning. Use a remote probe thermometer with the probe deep in the thigh to monitor temperatures.

Now just tuck the wing tips back behind the shoulders, and voilà!

Tip
Save the backbone for making homemade chicken stock.

HICKORY-SMOKED CHICKEN

Serves: 4   Prep Time: 30 minutes, plus brining time   Grill Time: 3 to 4 hours

1 whole chicken, spatchcocked

2 quarts NMT Basic Brine (page 18)

2 tablespoons NMT Basic BBQ Rub (page 14)

FOR THE MOP

1 cup apple cider vinegar

½ cup sweet smoky barbecue sauce

½ cup beer

1 tablespoon kosher salt

2 teaspoons ground black pepper

2 teaspoons hot sauce

1 teaspoon chili powder

1 teaspoon granulated garlic

1   Place the spatchcocked chicken in the brine and refrigerate for 6 to 8 hours.

2   Load your kamado with lump and mix in 3 or 4 chunks of hickory wood.

Preheat your kamado to 250°F and set it up for indirect heat.

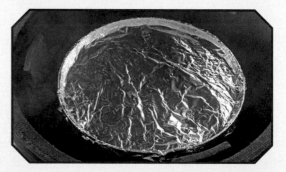

3   Make the mop by whisking all the ingredients together in a bowl. Set aside.

4   Remove the chicken from the brine, rinse, and thoroughly dry. Season with the rub on all sides; work some of the rub under the breast skin.

5   Once the smoke has changed from heavy white to "blue" or very light, place the chicken on the main grate, skin side up, and close the grill lid.

6. "Mop" the chicken every 30 to 45 minutes.

Work quickly to minimize the amount of time the grill is open. To avoid cross-contaminating the mop sauce after touching the not-fully-cooked chicken, I like to use a plastic squirt bottle to apply the mop. Quit mopping once the internal temperature in the breast reaches 150°F.

7   Smoke until the chicken reaches internal temperatures of 160°F–165°F in the breast and 175°F–180°F in the thighs. Remove from the grill, let rest for 10 minutes, and serve.

TRY THIS NEXT!

Try cooking a spatchcocked chicken using the raised direct method (Technique #28, page 114). Season with salt and lemon pepper and grill at 350°F, skin side up, for 1 hour.

#6

SMOKING, LOW AND SLOW

The kamado's fuel efficiency, moist cooking environment, and steady temperatures make it an ideal smoker for producing the most mouth-watering barbecue you've ever had. A 12-hour or longer cook might seem intimidating, but taking a few simple steps during setup will help ensure a trouble-free experience.

1 Start by cleaning your kamado. Remove and save the used coal. Clean out the ashes underneath the fire bowl. Also clean out any ashes between the base of the fire bowl and the sides. Make sure all vent holes are free of ash or small pieces of lump.

2 A word about wood: chips, chunks, or small splits all work in a kamado. Some people will swear by one or the other. Try for yourself and determine which works for you. Whatever you use, blend

it in throughout the coal, not just in one place; you should have wood in the top, bottom, and sides when you're done. Then top with your leftover used coal.

Generally I use four or five chunks of wood for a long cook. If using wood chips, I'll use about three cups. I don't soak mine first, I just mix them in with the coals. I like a blend of hickory and cherry, but use whatever hardwood, fruitwood, or blend that you like. Fill the fire bowl with wood and coal up to the top and you shouldn't have to worry about refueling even if the cook lasts 18 hours.

3   Have the kamado's heat deflector in place "legs up," with a drip pan on top of it and a cooking grate above that. If the drip pan rests directly on the heat deflector, it can get hot and burn drippings in the pan, creating foul smoke. To prevent that, raise the drip pan up a quarter inch with spacers and/or fill the pan ½ inch deep with water.

Preparing a pork butt

Pork butts come with a fat cap. Some folks get hung up on whether that fat cap should face up or down during the smoke. My answer is that it should be removed altogether. There's enough intramuscular fat to keep the meat moist and juicy. I find that you develop a better bark (that dark, tasty outside) by trimming off the fat cap, using a sharp boning knife.

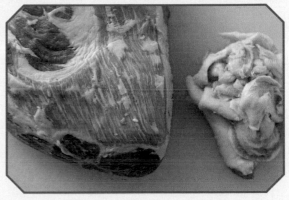

For BBQ, keep the meat cold until ready to cook; don't set it out to come to room temp. The longer the meat is on the smoker with an internal temperature of less than 140°F, the more prominent a smoke ring it will form. The smoke ring is that telltale pink color around the edges of smoked meats. It's not underdone; rather it is formed when myoglobin in the meat reacts with a nitrogen compound from the smoke. It doesn't dictate the amount of smoke flavor. You can have well-smoked meat with little or no smoke ring and it is possible to fake a smoke ring by using curing salts in their rub. Think of a smoke ring like grill marks — you can't taste it but you eat with your eyes first, right?

The cook

When you first light your kamado, you'll have a dense, thick white smoke, even after the dome temperature hits 250°F. Be patient and watch the smoke. After 30 to 45 minutes, it should change to a thin, almost bluish smoke, or even be completely clear. That signals that it's time to put the meat on. Even though you might not see the smoke, it's still there, working its magic.

Generally, 250°F is a good dome temperature for slow smoking. For a pork butt, plan on about 1½ hours per pound, though it can take as little as 1 hour or as long as 2 hours per pound. If I'm not in a hurry, I'll cook at 225°F for the first hour for the same reason I keep the meat cold until ready to cook — maximum smoke exposure.

Large cuts of meat like butts and briskets will often rise in temperature quickly but then hit a "stall point" and sit at 160°F–170°F for hours. If you're in a rush, you can push through the stall by wrapping the meat in foil or raising the cooking temperature to 275°F–300°F.

If the cooking temperature starts to drop several hours into the cook, you aren't running out of coal. Small pieces of lump are probably blocking air holes in your fire grate. Stick a wiggle rod through the lower vent, push the tip up through the holes, and give it a wiggle. This will cause loose ash and other blockages to dislodge, restoring circulation.

If you are smoking pork butts or brisket, it helps to rest them for longer than most cooked meats. Smoking enthusiasts refer to it as "FTC," which stands for foil-towel-cooler. Place towels in an empty cooler. Wrap the cooked meat in two layers of foil and place it in the cooler. Place more towels on top and then close the cooler for at least one hour but up to four. Not only does this let the meat rest, it holds it at temp; the meat will still be almost too hot to handle after four hours. This four-hour buffer certainly helps when cooking for company. It gives you time to make sure it is done well before guests expect to be fed.

About the slaw

The first time I was ever served slaw that contained tomatoes, I told the server that I'd ordered slaw, not salad. I mean, who puts tomatoes in slaw? I was told that it was "Carolina-style" slaw, vinegar-based with just a touch of diced tomato. Turns out, I liked it enough to make a version at home. The finishing sauce for the pork also has Carolina roots; it's a vinegar-based Piedmont style with a piquant kick.

SMOKED PORK BUTT WITH CAROLINA SLAW

Makes: 12 large or 16 regular-size pork sandwiches   Prep Time: 1 hour   Grill Time: 12 hours

8-pound bone-in pork butt, fat cap removed*

½ cup ground NMT Basic BBQ Rub, divided (page 14)

1 cup Lisbon-Style Vinegar BBQ Sauce (page 18)

12 to 16 plain hamburger buns

*This cut of pork was renamed "Boston roast" in 2013.

FOR THE CAROLINA SLAW

1 (1-pound) bag coleslaw mix

1 medium tomato, diced

2 tablespoons Lisbon-Style Vinegar BBQ Sauce (page 18)

1 teaspoon sugar

½ teaspoon kosher salt

1   Clean out your kamado and preheat it to 250°F. Set up for indirect heat as described above.

2   Reserve 1 tablespoon of the rub and use the rest to season the pork butt on all sides.

3   When the smoke changes from heavy white to very faint white, bluish, or clear, place the pork butt on the cooking grate. Close the lid and smoke until the pork reaches 195°F–197°F on a remote probe thermometer, about 1½ hours per pound.

Unlike what's required with other smokers, you never really need to open the lid to mop, add wood, or anything else.

4   Meanwhile, mix the slaw ingredients together in a bowl and refrigerate until ready to serve.

5   Fold a 48 x 18-inch length of aluminum foil in half, forming a 24 x 18-inch piece. Line a cooler with towels. When the pork reaches 195°F–197°F, carefully transfer the pork to the foil — watch out, it may try to fall apart on you. Wrap the foil tightly around the pork, place in the cooler, and top with more towels.

Sprinkle the reserved tablespoon of rub and 2 tablespoons of Lisbon-Style Vinegar BBQ Sauce over the shredded pork and toss to coat evenly.

7   Serve on the burger buns with the slaw and Lisbon sauce on the side.

Close the cooler and let the meat rest for at least 1 hour, or up to 4 hours.

6   Remove the meat from the cooler, unwrap, and transfer it to a cutting board. Use a pair of large forks, MeatRake shredders, "bear claws," or other implements of destruction to shred the pork into bite-size pieces.

SERVING TIP

Once your barbecue prowess becomes known, you will eventually be asked to cook for an event. When smoking pork butts, plan on ⅓ pound cooked meat per person. Divide the number of guests by 3 to figure out how much smoked pork you need, then double that to get the amount of raw pork butt you need. As an example, 25 guests ÷ 3 = 8.3 pounds of finished pork, or roughly 16 pounds of raw pork butt.

#7
SMOKING, HOT AND FAST

Lots of legends, lore, and lies come with all things barbecue. One canon tirelessly repeated by traditionalists was that for it to be considered barbecue, it had to be cooked low and slow.

But it was hard not to take notice when competitive BBQ cooks such as Mike Davis of Team Lotta Bull were out there winning major contests by smoking hot and fast. In the past five or six years, "turbo" smoking has become popular in BBQ forums for good reason: it significantly cuts the amount of time that's required.

The setup for hot and fast is just the same as for low and slow (page 40): clean your kamado, fill it with wood and coal, and set it up for indirect heat.

Preparing a brisket

Select a whole packer brisket that includes the flat and the point. Look for one that's USDA Choice or better, weighs 10 to 12 pounds, and is no more than 18 inches long, so it will fit in the kamado. Pick up the briskets to get a good feel for them. People might look at you strange but brisket picking is as much by feel as it is by sight.

Try to pick one with a thick but flexible flat section.

Trim the fat cap down to ⅛ inch thick; I use a sharp boning knife for this. I also aggressively trim out the hard fat between the flat and the point.

I use either a commercial beef injection (Butcher, FAB-B Lite, Kosmos Q) or one that I make myself.

The cook

Start with cold meat and cook it at 250°F for the first hour to give it maximum time to take on smoke.

I like to mop the meat about every 90 minutes when I cook hot and fast.

Insert a remote thermometer's probe into the brisket where the flat and point overlap.

Then open the bottom vent slightly more to bring the cooking temperature gradually up to 300°F over the course of about 30 minutes. Hold it there for the rest of the cook.

Hot spots are going to be more pronounced than when you smoke low and slow, since the kamado is at a higher temperature, so I put doubled foil under any meat that extends beyond the heat deflector.

The "stall" mentioned for low-and-slow smoking doesn't happen as often or for as long when I'm cooking hot and fast.

Even when starting off at a lower temperature as I do, this method lets me cook a brisket in 6 hours instead of 10 to 12 — and it's every bit as good as one smoked low and slow. You do have to keep a closer eye on your kamado; if the temperature gets away from you, this technique is less forgiving than low and slow. Meat smoked hot and fast benefits from a longer rest period, so I hold it in the cooler for at least two hours after it comes off the grill.

Here's how I like to cook my turbo briskets. I prefer to use oak wood, but feel free to use whatever you like. If you can't find the Bragg's Liquid Aminos, you can substitute soy sauce. The pan of stock below the brisket will catch drippings and make a beefy au jus.

TURBO BRISKET

Serves: 8 to 10   Prep Time: 1 hour   Grill Time: 6 to 7 hours

2 cups beef stock
10 to 12-pound packer beef brisket
3 tablespoons ground NMT Beef Rub (page 15)

FOR THE INJECTION
1 cup beef stock
1 tablespoon Bragg's Liquid Aminos

FOR THE MOP
1 cup beef stock
2 tablespoons hot sauce
2 tablespoons Worcestershire sauce
4 tablespoons (½ stick) unsalted butter
½ teaspoon finely ground NMT Beef Rub (page 15)
1 tablespoon sweet barbecue sauce

||||||||||||||||||||||||||||||||||||||||||||||||||||||||||||||||||||||||||||||||||||||||||||||||||||||||||||||||||||||||||||||

I   Clean your kamado, load it with lump and 4 or 5 chunks of wood, and preheat it to 250°F.

Set the heat deflector in place, legs up. Place spacers on the deflector, set the drip pan on the spacers, and pour 2 cups beef stock into the drip pan. Place the cooking grate on the heat deflector legs.

2   Trim the brisket (see above). Notice how the grain runs through the meat and mark one corner with a notch so you'll know how to slice the cooked meat.

3   In a small bowl, whisk together 1 cup beef stock and the Liquid Aminos to make the injection sauce. Inject into the brisket (see Technique #11, page 58) in a dozen or more places so that the entire brisket gets some of it.

Reserve ½ teaspoon of the rub and use the rest to season the brisket on all sides.

4 Place the mop ingredients in a small saucepan and bring to a simmer on the stovetop over medium-high heat. Mix well and turn off the heat.

5 When the smoke from the grill turns very light white, bluish, or clear, place the brisket on the cooking grate, fat side up. Protect the meat from any hot spots with foil. Close the dome and cook for 1 hour.

6 Flip the brisket so the fat cap faces down. Apply some of the mop. Slightly open the bottom vent (about ½ inch more on sliding vents) and gradually bring the temperature up to 300°F. Moisten the brisket with the mop sauce about every 90 minutes, or when the surface dries. When the internal temperature reaches 195°F, insert a metal skewer or temperature probe into the side of the brisket. If it feels like you're sticking it into butter, the brisket is ready to come off. If not, keep

cooking until it does — which could take until the internal temperature reaches 205°F.

7 Remove the brisket and wrap it tightly in aluminum foil. Transfer it to a towel-lined cooler and let rest for 2 to 4 hours.

8 Place the au jus from the drip pan in the freezer for 30 minutes, then scoop off and discard the fat layer that has formed on top. Warm the au jus on the stovetop over low heat.

9 Slice the brisket against the grain in pencil-thick slices. Serve with the warmed au jus.

TRY THIS NEXT!

To warm up leftover slices of brisket, place them in a shallow, oven-safe pan and pour in enough au jus to cover the bottom. Cover and place in a 300°F oven until warmed through, about 20 to 30 minutes.

#8

COOKING WINGS OVER DIRECT HEAT

Kamado grills are wing-making machines. Cooking them direct (page 27) is the fastest method, though it does require that you watch the wings carefully to avoid burning them. You can do them on the main cooking grid with the kamado running at 325°F–350°F or on a raised grid with the grill temperature at 350°F–375°F. Either way, cook for 15 minutes, flip, and cook another 15 minutes. If you're using a sauce, toss the cooked wings in the sauce, then put them back on the grill for 2 to 3 minutes.

To check for doneness, stick an instant-read thermometer into the thick portion of a drummette. Wings are done when they reach an internal temperature of 180°F.

A standard cooking grate can handle a four-pound family pack of wings, about 28 to 32 pieces when split into wingettes and drummettes.

What goes together better than hot wings and beer? Not much, so I used a beer brine for these wings to make sure they stay juicy in the high heat. The spiciness level as given here is medium. To reduce to mild, cut the hot sauce in half. For more spiciness, double it.

BEER-BRINED WINGS

Makes: 28 to 32 wing pieces   Prep Time: 30 minutes, plus 2 hours brining   Grill Time: 30 minutes

4 pounds chicken wings
1½ teaspoons garlic pepper seasoning
Celery, carrots, and ranch dressing, for serving

1 teaspoon red pepper flakes
2 cups cold beer

* If the wings will be in the brine for longer than 2 hours, reduce the salt and sugar to 2 tablespoons each.

FOR THE BEER BRINE
3 cups water
5 tablespoons kosher salt*
3 tablespoons sugar*
1 tablespoon dried minced garlic

FOR THE BUFFALO WING SAUCE
4 tablespoons (½ stick) unsalted butter
¼ cup hot sauce
½ teaspoon Worcestershire sauce

1 To make the brine, combine the water, salt, sugar, garlic, and red pepper flakes in a saucepan over high heat and bring to a boil. Remove from the stovetop and let cool for 10 minutes. Add the cold beer and refrigerate until the brine temperature is 40°F or below.

2 Cut the wings into pieces, discarding the wing tips or reserving them for making stock.

Place the wing pieces in the brine and refrigerate for 2 hours.

3 Remove the wings from the brine but *do not rinse*. Air-dry them on a rack over a baking sheet in the refrigerator for 1 hour.

4 Set up your kamado for raised direct heat (page 114) and preheat it to 375°F.

5   Meanwhile, make the buffalo sauce. Melt the butter in a small saucepan over medium heat, then whisk in the hot sauce and Worcestershire sauce. Keep warm on the stovetop over low heat.

6   Season the wings with the garlic pepper seasoning.

Place on the raised grate, close the lid, and cook for 15 minutes. Flip and cook for another 15 minutes.

7   Check the internal wing temperature. If it's 180°F or above, transfer the wings to a bowl, add the sauce, and toss to coat.

Return the wings to the grill just until the sauce sets, 2 to 3 minutes. Remove and serve with the obligatory celery, carrots, and ranch dressing. I'm pretty sure that's a state law.

TRY THIS NEXT!

Look up recipes for salt and vinegar wings and try one out with this cooking method. It's a good one for direct grilling because it doesn't use sugar (which burns). You can Google a recipe but basically you just season wings with Creole seasoning and seasoned salt before grilling them. Then in the last few minutes of grilling direct, give your cooked wings a dip in a vinegar and salt solution, and put them back on the grill for 3 to 5 minutes.

#9

30-20-10 WINGS

The 30-20-10 indirect method of cooking wings is easy to remember and more forgiving than direct heat for the time-challenged cook.

It's easy to remember because 30-20-10 is a mnemonic for the time intervals that you use. You set up the kamado for indirect heat (page 31) at 375°F. The wings cook for 30 minutes, you flip them over and cook for another 20 minutes, and then sauce and cook them for 10 more minutes.

I've mentioned that with the direct method for wings, you have to pay pretty close attention. People sometimes drink adult beverages when grilling wings, or so I've heard, and when people drink they sometimes forget to turn their wings. If you flip them 5 or 10 minutes late with the direct method, you may have some charred wings. But if you're using the 30-20-10 method and don't turn your wings for 40 minutes instead of 30, you're probably okay.

This process works well with just about any combination of rubs and sauces, even those that contain some sugar. (If you used this sticky wing recipe with direct heat, the sauce would probably burn in even two or three minutes.) You can also add wood to the lump for smoky wings.

If you're cooking on multiple grates — as with grid extenders, adjustable rigs, or Woo rings — you can just swap the top and bottom layers when you flip the wings at 30 minutes.

These Thai Sticky Wings are a refreshing change from the usual hot wings — sweet, spicy, and definitely finger-licking. The Chinese noodles might seem like just a garnish, but when you put out a platter of these wings and the sauce gets onto the crispy noodles, they become as addictive as the wings. If the Yoshida's sauce isn't available, substitute a sweet teriyaki sauce.

THAI STICKY WINGS

Makes: 28 to 32 wing pieces   Prep Time: 20 minutes   Grill Time: 1 hour

4 pounds chicken wings

2 cups wide Chinese crispy noodles

Chopped fresh cilantro, for garnish (optional)

FOR THE RUB

½ tablespoon kosher salt

⅓ teaspoon ground black pepper

⅓ teaspoon granulated garlic

½ teaspoon cornstarch

¼ teaspoon ground ginger

FOR THE SAUCE

½ cup red pepper jelly

¼ cup Mr. Yoshida's Original Gourmet Sauce

2 tablespoons cashew butter or peanut butter

2 tablespoons sriracha sauce

1½ teaspoons finely chopped fresh cilantro

I   Cut the wings into pieces, discarding the wing tips or reserving them for making stock.

Air-dry the wings by placing them on a rack set over a baking sheet and refrigerating for 1 hour.

2 Preheat the grill to 375°F. Set up your kamado for indirect heat with the heat deflector legs facing up.

Use a drip pan, or the sauce will make a burned mess of your deflector. Better yet, wrap the entire heat deflector with foil for this one.

3 Combine the dry rub ingredients in a small bowl. Season the wings with the rub, then place them on the grate, close the lid, and cook for 30 minutes.

4 While the wings are cooking, make the sauce. Combine the jelly, Yoshida's sauce, cashew or peanut butter, and sriracha in a saucepan over medium heat. Remove from the stovetop and stir in the cilantro.

5 Flip the wings, close the lid, and cook another 20 minutes.

6 Transfer the wings to a bowl, drizzle half the sauce over them, and toss to coat.

7 Return them to the grill for 10 more minutes with the lid closed and then remove from the heat.

8 Spread the crispy noodles on a platter, top with the wings, and drizzle on the remaining sauce. Garnish with cilantro if desired.

TRY THIS NEXT!

If you're not the type to create your own recipes, you can still have fun with this cooking method. Go to the grocery store and pick out a jarred rub and a sauce that seem like they'd go well together. Then use them for this technique. See? You just made your own recipe!

#10
ROASTING RACK/PAN COMBO

When you see a nice roast glistening with juices as it grills, it's sad to see that flavor drip off the meat to evaporate in the coals below. One way to retain the flavorful drippings is to use a roasting rack over a pan.

Typically you sear the roast over the flames to get the browning going and then place it on the rack. The pan underneath catches the drippings, adding flavor to whatever is already in the pan.

For beef roasts, I like beef stock in the pan with a crushed garlic clove or two and a sprig of fresh herbs, creating a smoky au jus to serve with the beef. With chicken and pork, I like diced root vegetables and a cup of stock in the pan.

A pan set directly over the coals will act as an indirect setup, but the pan bottom will get hot; it helps to use a thick pan such as stoneware. You need to stir veggies occasionally to keep them from burning, and keep an eye on the liquid in the pan to make sure it doesn't evaporate. It can be easier to use the rack/pan combo in indirect heat (page 31) with a heat diffuser or deflector protecting the pan bottom.

There are two common variations of the rack/pan technique. If you have multiple levels on your kamado (swing grate, adjustable rig, Woo, or raised grid), you can set the pan on the main grate and the meat on the higher grate above it. Another option is to use the root vegetables themselves as a "rack" and place the meat directly on them.

Root vegetables take about one hour to roast at 400°F. If your meat will take less time or needs to cook at a lower temperature, parboil the vegetables first so they will be fully cooked when your meat is ready.

Another trick that I like is to season the meat while it's on the rack above the vegetables. Any seasoning that falls through will just make your veggies taste all that much better.

Fire-Roasted Pork Loin with Root Vegetables

Serves: 4 to 6   Prep Time: 20 minutes   Grill Time: 1 hour, plus 10 minutes resting time

3-pound pork loin roast, trimmed and tied

1 pound Red Bliss potatoes, cut into 1-inch pieces

1 pound carrots, peeled and cut into 1-inch pieces

4 cloves garlic, peeled and slightly crushed

1 tablespoon canola oil

½ teaspoon kosher salt

½ teaspoon ground black pepper

½ cup chicken stock

For the Pork Rub

1 teaspoon kosher salt

1 teaspoon dried parsley

1 teaspoon ground black pepper

⅓ teaspoon turbinado sugar

½ teaspoon granulated garlic

½ teaspoon chili powder

½ teaspoon seasoned salt

1 Set up your kamado for direct heat and preheat it to 400°F.

2 Place the potatoes, carrots, and garlic in a medium bowl or gallon zip bag with the oil, salt, and pepper and toss to coat well. Place in a roasting pan, pour in the chicken stock, and set aside.

3 Mix the rub ingredients together in a small bowl. Season the pork roast with the rub on all sides. Remember to season it over the vegetables for "collateral seasoning."

4 Sear the roast over direct heat with the lid closed for 2 minutes per side.

5 Place a roasting rack in or above the pan of vegetables in the kamado; set the roast on the rack. Close the dome and cook until the roast reaches an internal temperature of 145°F, about 1 hour. Stir the vegetables occasionally.

6 Remove everything from the grill. Allow the roast to rest for 10 minutes, then slice and serve with the vegetables.

#11
INJECTING FLAVOR

Injecting solutions into meats for grilling is a way to add moisture and flavor without the long waiting times required for brines and marinades. Plus, it's sort of fun in a Nurse Ratched kind of way.

The type of solution depends on the meat. Butter-based injections work well for poultry, while fruit juice–based salty blends are good with pork. Beef stock mixes work well with beef, no surprise. You can buy a premade solution packaged with a plastic meat syringe, which is a good way to try it for the first time. Eventually you'll want to get a metal syringe, because the plastic ones will strip out with repeated use.

Many competitive BBQ teams use injections to amp up their flavor. Some even use phosphates in their injections to get an extra advantage, so it can get a little extreme. But simple homemade injections are my favorite. Use finely ground spices—it doesn't take much to clog the tip of your meat injector needle. Or use whole herbs that you can easily remove once you've cooked the flavor into the liquid, as in this recipe.

Agave-Glazed Smoked Turkey Breast

Serves: 4, with leftovers for Grilled Kentucky Hot Browns (page 112)   Prep Time: 45 minutes   Grill Time: 2½ hours

6 to 7-pound bone-in turkey breast

For the Injection
⅓ cup white wine

⅓ cup honey, preferably local

⅓ cup unsalted butter

1 or 2 sprigs fresh thyme

1 clove garlic, peeled and crushed

For the Rub
1 teaspoon garlic salt

1 teaspoon turbinado sugar

1 tablespoon smoked paprika

¾ teaspoon Creole seasoning

For the Glaze
¼ cup agave nectar

¼ cup chicken stock

2 tablespoons unsalted butter

1   Place the injection ingredients in a small saucepan, bring to a simmer over medium-low heat, and cook for 5 minutes. Remove from the stovetop and let cool for at least 30 minutes before you plan to inject.

2   Fill the fire bowl with lump coal and 4 fist-size chunks of hickory. Preheat to 300°F and set up for indirect.

3   Spatchcock the turkey breast (page 36) by cutting out the backbone with poultry sheers or a sharp knife and then pressing down firmly on the breastbone to flatten the breast.

4   Remove the herbs and garlic from the injection mixture. Fill a meat syringe and insert it into the turkey breast. Slowly draw out the needle while you apply gentle pressure, injecting the liquid into the meat.

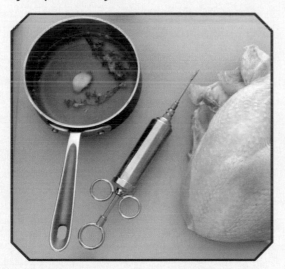

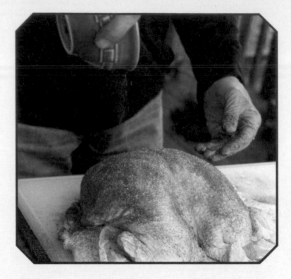

Repeat in 8 to 10 places across the breast.

6 Once the kamado is stable at 300°F and the smoke has turned clear or light white, place the turkey breast on the cooking grate skin side up. Cook with the lid closed until it reaches an internal temperature of 150°F.

7 While the turkey cooks, combine the glaze ingredients in a small saucepan over medium heat for 5 minutes. When the turkey breast's internal temperature reaches 150°F, brush on the glaze. Let the turkey cook until its temperature reaches 155°F–160°F, about 2 hours. Remove from the grill and let rest for 10 to 15 minutes before slicing.

5 Mix the rub ingredients together and sprinkle over the turkey breast.

TRY THIS NEXT!
Try injecting a pork butt with an injection based on either white grape juice or apple juice.

#12

USING BRINES

Dry meat is awful, isn't it? You chew and chew, but you feel like you're trying to swallow the Sahara Desert. Proper cooking is the best defense against dry meat, but using a brine is a good way to add flavor and retain moisture.

Foods that benefit from brines include low-fat pork roasts (such as loins and tenderloins), poultry, and fish. Yeah, despite the fact they've been swimming in saltwater all their lives, even ocean fish can use a brine. I normally don't brine fatty pork cuts (butts, ribs) or beef.

A brine is simply a solution of salt, sugar, and some type of aromatic. Just remember this one rule and you'll be on your way to making your own brines: use 2 to 5 tablespoons of kosher salt per quart of water and an equivalent amount (or less) of sugar. For brines under 4 hours, use more salt (3 to 5 tablespoons); for longer times, use 2 to 3 tablespoons.

If you have municipal water, consider using distilled water. Chlorine, fluoride, and whatever else is in city water isn't going to help the brine.

Add whatever aromatics you like. If they dissolve in water, then you don't have to heat your brine first. But a lot of seasonings (such as black pepper) aren't water soluble, and you need to heat the brine for 5 minutes to release their essential oils. Then you need to cool it back down to 40°F or below to make it food-safe. To do that, I put one of those blue freezer packs in a zip-top bag and put it in the brine in the refrigerator until the mixture comes down to temp.

It's your choice whether or not to rinse off the brine. If you don't, know that the meat will be salty, so you'll want to use low-salt rubs and seasonings for the cooking. Either way, make sure that you thoroughly dry the meat, because a damp surface will keep it from browning well.

For this brine, I leaned toward Tex-Mex, so for the sugar I used grated piloncillo, Mexican sugar cane. It has a rich caramel flavor that works great with pork. You could substitute brown sugar or sorghum. I gave the brine a little kick with ground aji panca chile, but you could switch it out with chipotle, ancho, or any favorite ground chile.

PORK TACOS WITH CORN SALSA

Serves: 4 to 6   Prep Time: 30 minutes, plus 6 to 8-hour brining   Grill Time: 30 minutes

2 pork tenderloins, trimmed of silver skin

12 corn tortillas

Taco toppings as desired (such as Mexican crema, cilantro, Cotija cheese)

FOR THE BRINE

1½ quarts distilled water

5 tablespoons kosher salt

4 tablespoons grated piloncillo (Mexican sugar)

½ teaspoon ground dried chile

½ teaspoon dried oregano

½ teaspoon dried minced garlic

½ teaspoon dried minced onion

FOR THE CORN SALSA

1½ cups corn kernels, drained if using canned

½ cup black beans, drained and rinsed

½ cup diced red onion

1 poblano chile, fire roasted, peeled, and seeds removed (see below)

¼ cup chopped fresh cilantro

Juice from 2 limes, preferably grilled

1 teaspoon kosher salt, or to taste

¼ teaspoon ground cumin

¼ teaspoon ground black pepper, or to taste

¼ teaspoon sugar

For the Rub

1½ teaspoons seasoned salt
1½ teaspoons chili powder

⅓ teaspoon granulated garlic
⅓ teaspoon dried oregano
½ teaspoon ancho chile powder

||||||||||||||||||||||||||||||||||||||||||||||||||||||||||||||||||||||||||||||||||||||||||||||||||||||||||||

1   Mix the brine ingredients together in a medium saucepan and bring to a strong simmer over medium-high heat. Remove from the stovetop and let rest for 15 minutes. Cool to 40°F by putting an ice bag in the brine and placing it in the freezer or fridge.

2   Remove the ice bag and place the pork in the brine. Refrigerate for 6 to 8 hours.

3   In a bowl, mix together all the salsa ingredients. Taste for seasoning and add salt and pepper as desired. Refrigerate until ready to serve.

4   Set up your kamado for direct heat and preheat it to 450°F.

5   Stir the rub ingredients together in a small bowl.

6   Remove the pork from the brine. Rinse, dry thoroughly, and season with the dry rub.

7   Place the tenderloins on the main grill grate and close the dome lid. Grill, turning every 5 minutes, until they reach an internal temperature of 145°F, about 25 to 30 minutes.

8   While you let the meat rest for 5 minutes, wrap the tortillas in a single stack in foil and warm them on the grill for about 20 seconds per side.

9   Slice the meat thinly and serve on the corn tortillas along with the salsa and any other toppings you wish.

GRILLED LIMES

To get an extra boost of flavor, try grilling citrus ingredients for marinades and cocktails. Cut them in half and grill direct, cut side down, over high heat for 2 to 3 minutes.

TRY THIS NEXT!

Boneless, skinless chicken breast halves benefit from a 4-hour brine. Try making your own signature brine for grilled chicken breasts. For salts, think about sea salt, garlic salt, and smoked salts. For sugar, don't forget about liquid forms such as molasses, sorghum, and agave nectar.

HOW TO FIRE-ROAST CHILES

Fire-roasting chiles softens their texture and creates a deep smoky flavor. You can buy them in cans and jars now but it only takes a few minutes to make your own. The best choices are chiles with thick flesh, like poblano, jalapeño, and bell "peppers." Thin-skinned chiles, like habanero, don't work well because they have almost no flesh left after scraping off the charred skins. **Tip:** The best tool for cleaning fire-roasted chiles is a grapefruit spoon with a serrated edge.

1 Set up your kamado for direct heat and preheat it to 450°F.

2 Place your chiles directly over the hottest part of the fire and allow to cook until blackened, about 2 to 3 minutes. You almost can't get them too dark, so don't worry. Repeat until all sides are charred.

3 Remove from the grill, place in a bowl, and cover the top with plastic. Allow to rest for 5 minutes, which steams the charred skins to loosen them. You can also use a paper lunch bag for this step.

4 Using a sharp knife, slice off the vine end of the chile, remove the seeds, and slice it lengthwise to flatten it out.

5 Use the knife edge or a serrated spoon to lightly scrape off the charred skins. Discard skins and use the roasted chile as needed.

#13

CREATING AND USING MARINADES

Marinating is similar to brining in that it adds moisture and flavor to meats, but marinades often also add a tenderizing effect to the meat's surface. While brines are combinations of liquid, salt, and seasonings, marinades typically consist of an acid, a fat, and seasonings.

Marinades are easy and cost effective to whip up at home. Just use one part acid for every two to three parts oil or fat and then add seasonings. Common acids include vinegar, citrus juice, tea, liquor, buttermilk, and Greek yogurt. Avoid pineapple—it contains the enzyme bromelain, which can turn proteins to mush. For the fat, high-heat oils such as peanut and canola seem to work best for grilling. The seasoning possibilities are endless. And with an oil base, you don't normally have to heat the marinade; most spices will release their flavors more readily than in a water-based solution.

If you don't care to create your own recipes, there are plenty of good marinades and marinade mixes on the grocery shelves and online. Producers do a good job of staying on top of food trends. Just don't trust any claims for 30-minute marinades; every one that I've tried would have benefited from two or three more hours.

How long to marinate depends on the type and size of your meat, but four to eight hours is typical except for delicate items like seafood. Marinades will only penetrate the surface, regardless of how long you leave meat in the marinade, so there's no benefit in marinating for extremely long times (12 to 24 hours). There are devices that claim to shorten marinating times by vacuum-sealing the meat and marinade together.

Meat doesn't have to be submerged in marinade, just coated, so my favorite tool is a zip-top plastic bag. This way you only need 1/3 to 1/2 cup marinade per pound of meat. Avoid reactive metal containers such as aluminum or cast iron.

Be sure to pat your meat dry before grilling; moist surfaces are the enemy of the Maillard reaction that creates the flavorful brown crust we associate with grilling. Besides, oil dripping into hot coals results in sooty smoke.

Regardless of where I am, there's something about jerk chicken that makes me feel like my feet are in the sand and I can smell ocean air. This marinade uses citrus for its acid and a lot of seasonings found in jerk chicken rubs. Instead of the traditional bone-in chicken, the recipe calls for butterflied chicken breast that can be eaten as an island-style sandwich. Our local produce department stocks an array of dried chiles, but if you can't find the dried habanero, you can substitute either a seeded and finely diced fresh habanero or 1/2 teaspoon cayenne pepper.

Island-Style Chicken Sandwich

Serves: 4   Prep Time: 30 minutes, plus 4 to 6 hours marinating   Grill Time: 15 minutes

4 chicken breast halves, boneless and skinless

4 Kaiser rolls

2 tablespoons unsalted butter, melted

Lettuce, tomato, onion, or other sandwich fillings of your choice

For the Marinade

3 tablespoons orange juice

1 tablespoon lime juice

½ teaspoon dried oregano

1 tablespoon dark brown sugar

⅛ teaspoon ground allspice

¼ teaspoon ground dried habanero chile

¼ teaspoon ground cinnamon

1 whole clove

1 clove garlic, chopped

⅛ teaspoon ground ginger

¼ teaspoon dried thyme leaves

½ teaspoon onion salt

½ cup peanut oil

1   In a bowl, whisk together all the marinade ingredients except the peanut oil. Slowly add the oil while whisking rapidly.

2   Butterfly the chicken breasts. Place a half breast on a cutting board and remove the loose tenderloin, if still attached. Press down with the palm of your non-cutting hand and *very carefully* use a boning knife to slice through from one side of the breast to within ½ inch of the other side.

Open the breast like a book and press flat. Repeat for the other half breasts.

3   Place the butterflied breasts and any tenderloins in a zip-top plastic bag. Add the marinade, seal, and refrigerate for 4 to 6 hours, flipping the bag over occasionally.

4   Set up your kamado for direct heat and preheat it to 400°F.

5   Remove the chicken from the marinade and pat dry. Grill with the lid closed until the chicken reaches an internal temperature of 160°F, about 5 to 7 minutes per side depending on the thickness of the breasts. Remove from the grill and let rest for 5 minutes.

6   Scrub the grill grate with a brush or a ball of foil to remove the debris. Split the rolls and lightly brush the insides with the melted butter. Grill cut side down until crispy and toasted.

7   Serve the chicken on the toasted rolls with your chosen accompaniments.

TRY THIS NEXT!
Make your own marinade. If you're stuck for ideas, just make the oil/acid base and then whisk in some type of prepared pesto—instant marinade!

14

DUTCH OVENS

A Dutch oven can be extremely useful on a kamado grill. You can use it for braised dishes such as milk-braised pork shoulder, soups, stews, chilies, breads, and yes, even dessert.

Any Dutch oven can work, but I prefer plain black cast iron; the enamel-coated ones tend to show a smudgy film when used in a smoky environment. Flat-bottom Dutch ovens work well when setting the Dutch oven on a cooking grate—for example, if cooking with direct heat. If I am cooking indirect and place the Dutch oven on the heat deflector, I like the camp-style Dutch oven with the legs on the bottom. The legs keep the bottom of the Dutch oven from getting overheated from sitting on a hot heat deflector.

Many dishes start with browning meats. To do that, use the Dutch oven over direct heat on the main cooking grate at 325°F–350°F. Browning meat requires the lid to be open much of the time, which can get your coals burning and drive up your temperatures, so I completely shut the bottom vent during the browning phase. Just don't forget to open it when you shut the lid to finish cooking.

For long-simmering dishes, there are several options. You can switch to indirect heat, which involves some up-front work but minimizes how often you have to open the kamado to stir. Another option is to elevate the Dutch oven on a raised grid, reducing the heat from below. A third possibility is to remain over direct heat but shut the lower vents substantially to lower the temperature. Liquid evaporates quickly in a hot kamado, so I generally simmer with the Dutch oven lid on.

This recipe is a variation of one my mom taught me to make at Cades Cove Campground in the Smoky Mountains. It started out as a dessert, but I've changed it around a little to make it into a breakfast dish. The parchment paper isn't required, but it sure makes cleanup easier!

CHERRY CHEESE DANISH COBBLER

Serves: 6 to 8   Prep Time: 15 minutes   Grill Time: 45 minutes to 1 hour

4 ounces cream cheese, cut in 12 to 15 pieces

2 (22-ounce) cans cherry pie filling

1½ cups sugar

⅓ cup self-rising flour

⅓ cup whole milk

6 tablespoons (⅓ stick) unsalted butter, melted

1 Preheat your kamado to 350°F and set it up for indirect cooking. You can also use convection baking (page 72) for this recipe.

2 Cut a piece of parchment paper into a circle 1 to 2 inches larger all around than the bottom of an 8-quart Dutch oven. An easy way to do this is to fold the parchment in half twice, then cut an arc opposite the folded corner. Voilà...

circle! Line the bottom of the Dutch oven with the parchment circle.

3   Place the cream cheese pieces around the bottom of the pan and then pour in the pie filling.

4   In a bowl, whisk together the sugar, flour, milk, and melted butter. Drizzle over the pie filling.

5   Place the Dutch oven on the main grate if using indirect heat, or directly on the heat deflector or pizza stone if using convection baking. Bake with the Dutch oven uncovered and grill lid closed until the top is golden brown, about 45 minutes to 1 hour.

TRY THIS NEXT!

Try making a braised recipe in a Dutch oven. Osso buco, chicken cacciatore, and adobo all work well in Dutch ovens.

#15

CONVECTION BAKING

The unique design of the kamado lets you set it up to create hot air currents and use it like a convection oven. Why would you want to do that? Convection cooking offers even heat distribution and shorter cooking times.

To set up for convection baking, you have two options. Either way, preheat your kamado to the desired cooking temperature. For the first option, insert a heat deflector with the legs down. For the second, place the heat diffuser in the grill and then place a pizza stone on the cooking grate. Both of

these setups allow currents of air to flow up into and around the cooking area, creating convective currents.

Despite the kamado's being the most even cooking grill that I have used, it's still a good idea to rotate your food halfway through the anticipated baking times. For better browning on top, move your food higher up in the kamado to benefit from heat reflecting off the dome lid.

This dessert gets its unique kick from the pride and joy of the Appalachian region—moonshine. When I first started cooking with moonshine, I had to get it from someone "who knew a guy" here in the foothills of the Smoky Mountains. But laws have changed, moonshine has gone corporate, and you can buy it from a package store in most states. The alcohol will burn off during the flambé, but if you prefer, you can substitute apple cider for the moonshine and skip the flambé part.

APPALACHIAN APPLE FLAMBÉ

Serves: 6   Prep Time: 15 minutes   Grill Time: 45 minutes

6 frozen puff pastry shells

5 tablespoons unsalted butter, divided

6 Granny Smith apples, peeled, cored, and cut into 12 wedges each

½ cup packed light brown sugar

¼ teaspoon apple pie spice

¼ cup apple pie-flavored moonshine (70 proof or higher)

Sweetened whipped cream, for serving

FOR THE BOOTLEGGER CARAMEL SAUCE

¼ cup water

1 cup sugar

½ cup heavy cream

½ teaspoon salt

1 tablespoon apple pie-flavored moonshine

1   To make the caramel sauce on the stovetop, stir the water and sugar together in a thick-bottomed pan over medium heat and cook for 5 minutes, continuing to stir occasionally. Increase the heat to medium-high and continue cooking, stirring frequently. When amber in color, remove from the heat and slowly add the cream while whisking. Whisk in the salt and moonshine. Pour into a jar and let cool.

2   Set up your kamado grill for convection baking as described above and preheat it to 425°F. Place the puff pastry shells on a pizza stone or baking rack and set it on the heat deflector or grill grate. Close the lid and bake until raised and golden, 20 to 25 minutes.

3 Remove the heat deflector or diffuser and switch the grill to direct heat. Preheat a grill-safe pan in the kamado for 10 minutes.

4 Add 2 tablespoons of the butter to the pan, then add the apples and sauté, tossing occasionally, until the apple slices are tender, about 12 to 13 minutes, keeping the dome lid closed as much as possible. Add the sugar, apple pie seasoning, and remaining butter and toss or stir to combine. Cook another 2 to 3 minutes, until the sauce reaches the consistency of syrup.

5 Be sure to use the safety precautions on page 7 as you flambé the dessert. Carefully warm the moonshine on the grill in a small, grill-safe saucepan. Remove the pan with the apples from the grill, pour moonshine over the apples, and return the pan to the grill. Hold a lit wand-style lighter or long match just over the pan to quickly ignite the mixture while the alcohol vapors rise. Let the alcohol burn off, about 1 minute. Cover with the pan lid to make sure the flames are extinguished. Remove from the grill.

6 Top the cooked pastry shells with the apple mixture. Drizzle with the caramel sauce and top with whipped cream.

TIP
Reheat the caramel sauce in a double boiler to make it easy to pour. You can make a no-cook version of the caramel sauce by combining ½ cup store-bought caramel syrup, 1 teaspoon apple pie moonshine, and a pinch of apple pie seasoning.

#16

SEAR/ROASTING STEAKS AND CHOPS

Think of three words to describe a steak. I'll bet one of the words was "thick." Almost everyone loves a thick and juicy steak. But if you're grilling a 1½-inch or thicker steak, by the time the middle is cooked, the outside will be burned to a crisp. There are two common methods for perfectly cooking a thick steak on a kamado grill. One is the sear/roast technique (also known as "TRex") and the other is roast/sear (also known as "reverse sear," page 78). Both

involve cooking in two stages, and both result in steaks that are evenly cooked from edge to edge.

Sear/roast lets you avoid handling hot ceramics in the middle of the cook. It also makes it easier to nail the exact internal temperature that you want, since you approach it slowly instead of heading straight for it over raging coals.

The method is simple. Start with a very hot grill and sear your steak over direct heat (page 27) briefly on both sides. Remove the steak and switch the kamado to an indirect setup (page 31). Close down the bottom and top vents so they're barely open to drop the temperature into the 300°F–350°F range. Then put the steak back on and let it roast until it hits your desired final internal temperature. Because the steak finishes with a slow roast, the rest period cooking will be less drastic, about 5°F added to your final temperature on the grill.

The TRex method is similar but doesn't use the indirect setup; instead, it finishes directly but at the lower roasting temperature. This means that it's being heated mostly from below, which can mess up the even cooking you're looking for. That's why I prefer finishing with an indirect setup—it evens out the direction of heat without my having to flip the steak during the roast.

A cowboy ribeye is another name for a ribeye with the rib bone still in. It's a really big steak, weighing up to two pounds—just right for the sear/roast approach. A steak like this is meant for more than one person and is often served on a platter, cut from the bone into 1-inch slices. But if you have the appetite of a cowboy, you could eat this hunk of beef in one sitting...as my older son did.

Cowboy Ribeye with Ranch-Style Beans

Serves: 2 to 3 people (or 1 person with a really big appetite)   Prep Time: 20 minutes   Grill Time: 1 hour

1 cowboy ribeye beef steak, 1½ to 2 pounds

2 teaspoons coarsely ground NMT Beef Rub (page 15)

½ teaspoon finely ground NMT Beef Rub, for finishing

For the Ranch-Style Beans
1 slice bacon

2 tablespoons diced red bell pepper

½ tablespoon finely diced, seeded jalapeño chile

1 (15-ounce can) pinto beans, drained and rinsed

1½ tablespoons water

1½ tablespoons tomato paste

½ teaspoon chili powder

½ teaspoon light brown sugar

¼ teaspoon kosher salt

¼ teaspoon ground black pepper

¼ teaspoon ground cumin

Large pinch of chopped fresh cilantro

1 Set up your kamado for direct heat and preheat it to 450°F.

2 Crisp the bacon in a small sauté pan on the stovetop over medium-high heat. Remove, reserving 1 tablespoon of the bacon grease in the pan.

3 Sauté the bell and jalapeño chile in the pan for 3 minutes, stirring occasionally. Add the remaining ingredients for the ranch-style beans, reduce heat to medium, and bring to a simmer.

4 Open your grill vents and bring the temperature up to 550°F–600°F. While the temperature is coming up, season the steak with the 2 teaspoons coarsely ground NMT Beef Rub.

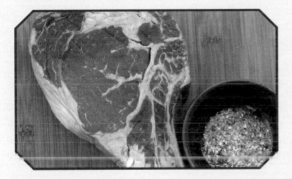

If the beans get to bubbling too much, take them off until Step 6.

5 Grill the steaks with the lid closed 2 minutes per side, turning a quarter turn at the 1-minute mark on each side. Remove the steaks from the grill.

6 Carefully remove the hot grill grate and set up the grill for indirect cooking. If you took the beans off, return them to the kamado now. Close the vents so they're barely open to drop the cooking temperature to 300°F–350°F. This might take 10 to 15 minutes, but don't worry—your steak will be fine and is actually still cooking. The internal temperature of the meat will raise about 10° during this time.

7 Place a remote thermometer probe in the steak and return it to the kamado. Cover and slow roast until the steak reaches 125°F for medium-rare or 135°F for medium, about 30 minutes. Remove the steak and the beans.

8 Season the steak with the ½ teaspoon finely ground beef rub and allow to rest for 5 minutes. Serve alongside the beans.

#17
REVERSE SEARING STEAKS AND CHOPS

The reverse sear technique is an extremely reliable way to get evenly cooked and juicy steaks and chops, every time. If you want your steak medium-rare, it will be medium-rare from one edge to the other—unlike direct grilling, which gives you a medium-rare center surrounded by a layer of medium and another of well done.

The Primo barbecue forum was one of the first groups to embrace this technique

when Chris Finney of the Iron Pig BBQ team began promoting the method a little over a decade ago. Now it has spread among kamado users everywhere.

The process is simple—and the opposite of the sear/roast procedure (page 75). Start with a slow roast on a kamado set up for indirect heat at 250°F, cooking your meat until it's 5° under your desired final internal temperature. (If you like, you can include wood in the coals for more pronounced smoke notes.) This part usually takes 45 minutes to an hour, but go by the temperature. Remove the meat and let it rest while you remove the heat deflector to switch the kamado to direct heat (see notes on handling a hot heat deflector in Fire Safety, page 7). Open the bottom and top vents to let the temperature shoot upwards of 500°F, then put the meat back on just long enough to sear the outside, about 1 to 1½ minutes a side.

The reverse sear method absolutely rocks for one-inch or thicker steaks and chops, like these Two-Finger Pork Chops. They're called "two-finger" because that's how you know they're thick enough when you're at the grocery store. The chop should be at least as thick as your index and middle fingers together, turned sideways. I was taught that when a grilling mentor sent me to the store to get supplies during a cookout way back when, and it has stuck with me ever since.

TWO-FINGER PORK CHOPS

Serves: 4   Prep Time: 30 minutes, plus 2 to 4 hours brining   Grill Time: 1 hour

4 porterhouse pork chops, *at least* 1 inch thick

2 quarts NMT Basic Brine (page 18)

½ teaspoon ground black pepper

¼ teaspoon cayenne pepper

FOR THE RUB

1 tablespoon smoked paprika

2 teaspoons turbinado sugar

2 teaspoons kosher salt

2 teaspoons light brown sugar

⅓ teaspoon granulated garlic

FOR THE GLAZE

⅓ cup red pepper jelly

2 tablespoons sorghum syrup

1 tablespoon unsalted butter

1½ teaspoons soy sauce

IIIIIIIIIIIIIIIIIIIIIIIIIIIIIIIIIIIIIIIIIIIIIIIIIIIIIIIIIIIIIIIIIIIIIIIIIIIIIIIIIIIIIIIIIIIIIIIII

1   Place the pork chops in the brine and refrigerate for 2 to 4 hours.

2   Preheat your kamado to 250°F and set it up for indirect heat. If you add wood for extra smoke flavor, wait for the smoke to change from heavy white to light white, bluish, or clear.

3   Remove the pork chops from the brine, rinse, and pat dry.

4 Mix the rub ingredients together in a small bowl. Season the pork chops with the rub on all sides.

Place on the grill and roast with the grill lid closed until the chops hit an internal temperature of 140°F–145°F.

5 Meanwhile, combine the glaze ingredients in a small saucepan over medium heat on the stovetop for 5 minutes, stirring occasionally and remove from heat.

6 Remove the chops from the grill and let rest on a raised rack. Switch the kamado to direct heat and open the top and bottom vents to bring the cooking temperature to above 500°F.

7 Return the chops to the grill and sear for 1½ minutes a side. Brush with the glaze and remove to serve.

TRY THIS NEXT!
Give the reverse sear method a whirl with super-thick strip steaks.

18

REVERSE SEARING ROASTS

The reverse sear technique works equally as well for roasts as for steaks and chops. A pork loin or a tied-and-rolled pork shoulder roast comes out dripping with savoriness. It's a can't-fail technique for whole beef tenderloin, tri-tip, or ribeye roast.

The process is mostly the same as for steaks and chops, with an indirect setup at a cooking temperature of 250°F and a 500°F-plus finishing sear, as described in the previous section. One difference is that most roasts will cook considerably longer than steaks and chops. If the cook will take longer than an hour, it's a good idea to flip the roast about halfway through. You also might want to use a roasting pan/rack combination (see page 55) to capture the drippings for a gravy, sauce, or au jus.

What do you do when you have a gorgeously cooked medium-rare prime rib and a guest who prefers medium-well or well done? Trick them! Place their slice in a pan of barely simmering beef stock for one minute per side, and the pink will disappear.

This beef tri-tip roast is ideal for practicing the reverse sear method. The three-chile rub creates a spicy mahogany crust that balances the mild, beefy interior. You can make the salsa verde a day or two ahead. Serve the tri-tip as a roast, cut into pencil-wide slices, or slice it thin and serve with Cilantro-Lime Rice (page 105), refried beans, and corn tortillas. Either way, it's delicious!

THREE-CHILE TRI-TIP WITH GRILLED SALSA VERDE

Serves: 4 to 6   Prep Time: 1 hour   Grill Time: 1 hour 40 minutes

2 to 3-pound beef tri-tip

FOR THE SALSA VERDE
1 pound tomatillos, peeled

1 jalapeño chile

1 poblano chile

1 onion, peeled and sliced

1 teaspoon minced garlic

2 tablespoons beef stock

¼ cup chopped fresh cilantro

Kosher salt and ground black pepper to taste

FOR THE RUB
⅓ teaspoon garlic salt

¼ teaspoon ground cumin

¼ teaspoon onion powder

¼ teaspoon dried oregano

¼ teaspoon dried parsley

¼ teaspoon ancho chile powder

¼ teaspoon chipotle chile powder

⅛ teaspoon cayenne pepper

1   To free yourself from last-minute tasks, make the salsa verde ahead of time. Char the tomatillos, jalapeño and poblano chiles, and onion slices over direct heat at 450°F until blackened on all sides, about 5 minutes. You can cook the onions directly on the grill grates as rings or cook them on a griddle as shown in the picture. The grill grates

will give you more char; the griddle yields a more tender onion.

Transfer to a bowl, cover with plastic wrap, and let rest 5 minutes. Peel and seed the chiles and place in a blender along with the tomatillos, onion, garlic, beef stock, and cilantro. Pulse several times until the mixture has the consistency of salsa. Pour into a small saucepan and simmer on the stovetop for 5 minutes; season to taste with salt and pepper. Let cool, then cover and refrigerate until ready to use.

2   To cook the tri-tip, preheat the kamado to 250°F and set up for indirect heat with the heat deflector in "legs up," a drip pan, and cooking grate.

3   Mix the rub ingredients together in a small bowl. Season the tri-tip with the rub all over.

4   Once the smoke has turned clear or light, place the roast on the cooking grate and slow roast with the lid closed until it reaches an internal temperature of 100°F. Flip the roast and continue cooking with the lid closed until it reaches 127°F for medium-rare, or 5°F less than your desired finishing temperature (see Temperatures for Cooking Meat, page 13). Remove from the grill and place on a rack to rest.

5   Switch the kamado setup to direct heat by removing the deflector and drip pan. Open the top and bottom vents to bring the cooking temperature up to above 500°F.

6 Sear the roast on the top and bottom for 2 minutes each. To sear the edges, use tongs to hold the roast on its side for about 30 seconds for each edge.

Remove from the grill and allow to rest for 5 minutes, then slice and serve.

TRY THIS NEXT!

For your next holiday meal, try reverse searing a whole beef tenderloin on your kamado. Just ask your butcher to trim and tie it and then season it simply with kosher salt, cracked black pepper, and granulated garlic. The slow roast period should take about 45 to 60 minutes.

#19
HOT-TUBBING

The "hot-tubbing" technique is a poor man's sous-vide. Instead of a fancy sous-vide machine, all you need is a quality fast-response thermometer. This method popped up on an online kamado forum several years ago and seemed to spread from there.

The point of hot-tubbing is similar to that of sous-viding (page 136) and reverse-searing: evenly cooked food. People often recommend tempering meat by leaving it at room temperature for some time. Water transfers heat more efficiently than air, so

submerging the meat in warm water makes sense. With a bunch of guys grilling and drinking beer together on a deck with a hot tub, it was bound to happen. Someone put a steak in a zip-top bag and stuck it in the hot tub prior to grilling, and the rest is history.

This trick is simple. You seal steaks or chops in a plastic bag and submerge them in hot water for an hour before grilling. You want water warming the meat, not air, so use vacuum-sealing or press as much air as you can out of a zip-top bag. Your water should be 105°F–115°F for the entire time, and there are several ways to achieve that:

- Use a hot tub (I just can't help but worry about a hole in the bag letting a little water in and...just *ewwww*).

- Use very hot tap water in a six-pack cooler, monitoring the temperature and adding hot water as needed.

- Use a large pot of hot water on a stove burner, adjusting the heat to keep the water temperature in the right low range.

To finish, you grill your meat over high heat until the internal temperature hits the desired mark. Since your meat is above 100°F to start, the grilling time will be much shorter than normal.

FLAT IRON STEAK TACOS WITH GREEN CHILE CREMA

Serves: 4 to 6   Prep Time: 20 minutes, plus 1 hour soaking   Grill Time: 15 minutes

1 flat iron steak, about 1 pound

2 or 3 bell peppers (different colors), seeded and cut into strips

1 large sweet onion, peeled and cut into strips

8 to 12 corn tortillas

1 tablespoon peanut or corn oil

1 teaspoon garlic salt

½ teaspoon ground black pepper

FOR THE STEAK RUB

1 teaspoon seasoned salt

½ teaspoon granulated garlic

½ teaspoon chili powder

¼ teaspoon ancho chile powder

¼ teaspoon ground cumin

¼ teaspoon ground black pepper

¼ teaspoon dried oregano

FOR THE GREEN CHILE CREMA

¼ cup canned, diced green chiles

¼ cup Mexican crema or sour cream

1 tablespoon chopped fresh cilantro

½ teaspoon sugar

¼ teaspoon red pepper flakes

¼ teaspoon ancho chile powder

¼ to ½ teaspoon salt to taste

2 limes

1 **Score the steak on both sides in a crisscross pattern. Mix together the rub ingredients in a small bowl and use to season the steak on both sides.** Vacuum-seal the steak in a plastic bag or place in a zip-top bag with the air pressed out. Submerge in 105°F–115°F water for up to 1 hour.

2   Place the bell peppers and onion in a medium bowl and toss to coat with oil, garlic salt, and black pepper.

3   In a small bowl, combine all the green chile crema ingredients except for the lime. Cover and refrigerate.

4   Set up your kamado for direct grilling and preheat it to 450°F.

5   Cut the limes in half and grill them, cut side down, for 2 to 3 minutes. Stir up to 2 tablespoons juice from the grilled limes into the green chile crema.

6   Remove the steak from the water and its package. Grill until it reaches an internal temperature of 127°F for medium-rare, about 2 to 3 minutes per side. (For medium, cook to 132°F.) If you want appealing crosshatch marks, rotate the steak a quarter turn halfway through each side's grilling time. Transfer to a resting rack.

7   Place a vegetable wok, basket, or grill topper (page 104) on the grill.

Add the bell pepper and onion strips and cook, tossing occasionally, until slightly charred and softened, about three to five minutes. Remove from the grill.

8   Grill the tortillas directly on the grill until they warm and start to brown a little, just 10 to 15 seconds per side. If you aren't comfortable doing this, you can stack them in groups of 4, wrap them in foil, and heat directly on the grill until warmed through, about 30 seconds a side.

9   Slice the steak and serve it on the tortillas with the grilled vegetables and green chile crema.

TRY THIS NEXT!
Try hot-tubbing ribeye steaks and serving them with oyster mushrooms that you've sautéed in garlic butter.

#20
STUFFED CHEESEBURGERS

Originating as the "Jucy Lucy" in St. Paul, Minnesota, the stuffed burger trend has swept the nation with restaurants and backyard chefs all giving it their own spin. Stuffed cheeseburgers are an entertaining way to show your creative flare on the grill.

There are plenty of tools for sale that claim to take the hassle out of making stuffed burgers. Some work, some don't — but frankly, sticking a couple of burger patties together with stuff in the middle just isn't that difficult. Take a three-ounce burger patty, put your stuffing mix on it, top it with a second three-ounce patty, and then seal the edges by kneading them together. Boom. It does help to keep the burger meat quite cold while you're working with it.

The stuffing mix can be anything that sounds good to you, but here are some ideas:

- Bacon, Cheddar cheese, and smoky barbecue sauce

- Sun-dried tomatoes and Monterey Jack cheese

- Marsala-sautéed mushrooms and Swiss cheese

- Caramelized onions and blue cheese

Grilling stuffed burgers isn't any different than grilling thick regular burgers. Grilling them direct at 400°F for about four minutes per side does the trick, but check your temperatures, as always. If you suffer a "blowout" and one or more of your burgers starts to ooze cheese, don't stress. That's not a defect, it's character!

GREEN CHILE–STUFFED BURGERS WITH AVOCADO RANCH DRESSING

Serves: 4   Prep Time: 20 minutes   Grill Time: 10 minutes

1½ pounds ground round
1½ teaspoons NMT Burger Mix-in (page 16)
4 hamburger buns
2 tablespoons unsalted butter, melted

FOR THE AVOCADO RANCH DRESSING
⅓ cup prepared ranch dressing
¼ cup diced avocado
¼ teaspoon ancho chile powder

FOR THE STUFFING MIXTURE
2 ounces cream cheese, softened
¼ cup canned diced green chiles
¼ cup shredded Colby Jack cheese

1 To make the dressing, place the ranch dressing, diced avocado, and chile in a blender and pulse until smooth. Refrigerate in a sealed container until ready to use. You can make this up to 2 days in advance.

2 Mix the ground round with the NMT Burger Mix-in. Divide the mixture into 8 (3-ounce) burger patties.

3 In a small bowl, mix together the cream cheese, diced chiles, and cheese for the stuffing.

4   Top **4** meat patties with spoonfuls of the cheese mixture.

Crown with the remaining **4** patties. Seal the edges of each stuffed burger by pinching or kneading them together — like kneading clay — and then smooth over the seam with your finger.

5   Set up your kamado grill for direct heat and preheat it to 400°F.

6   Cook the burgers **4** minutes per side and remove from the grill.

7   Lightly brush the insides of the buns with the melted butter. Place on the grill grate, buttered side down, until toasted, just a few seconds.

8   Serve the burgers on the buns with a slather of avocado ranch dressing.

TRY THIS NEXT!
How about a Stuffed-Burger Roulette Party? Set up an ingredient bar so everyone can make their own stuffed burger mix. After the burgers have all cooked on the grill, have everyone select one at random with no clue as to what's inside.

#21
STIR-FIRING

Stir-frying is a high-heat cooking method. Kamados push out some serious heat. Stir-frying and fire naturally come together for "stir-firing." The great thing about stir-firing is that it's so fast, you can stir-fire a side dish in the time it takes for the main course to rest. Someone could write an entire book about stir-firing on the grill, but here are some quick tips for getting started:

Wok 'n' roll

The cornerstone of stir-firing is a good wok. For the kamado, carbon steel works the best for me. To use a round-bottom wok, you'll need to get a Spider rig or similar frame to support the wok on the fire ring. Flat-bottom woks can be used directly on the main grate, with or without a Spider rig. Choose a wok with a small metal hoop-style handle on each side; long-handled woks don't fit in the kamado with the lid closed.

Mise en place

Stir-firing happens so quickly that you need to have everything you'll be using within arm's reach. Also make sure that all your ingredients are dried off well. Wet ingredients result in mushy stir-fired dishes.

Fire management

Stir-firing requires the wok top to be open most of the time, so a bed of hot coals can become a fully engaged fire in minutes. As long as the lid is open, keep the bottom vent fully closed to minimize runaway fires. The temperatures will rise while you stir-fire with the lid open, so try to start on the lower end, about 375°F–400°F, so you're done cooking by the time the temperature gets to 500°F or so.

The summery colors and flavors of Basil Fried Rice make it a first-rate side dish for Thai-seasoned flank steak — and you can cook it while the steak rests. You should be able to find whole red chiles in the Latino section of your grocery store, but if not, you can substitute a ½ teaspoon of red pepper flakes. The cashew butter used to be difficult to find, but now one of the big peanut butter companies (think "choosy moms") sells it nationwide. If you can't find it, just use peanut butter.

THAI BEEF WITH BASIL FRIED RICE

Serves: 4 to 6   Prep Time: 30 minutes, plus 4 to 6 hours marinating   Grill Time: 20 minutes

1½ to 2-pound flank steak, scored on both sides

FOR THE MARINADE
2 tablespoons lime juice

2 tablespoons fish sauce

2 tablespoons oyster sauce

¼ cup peanut oil

1 teaspoon sesame oil

1 teaspoon red pepper flakes

1 teaspoon minced fresh ginger

2 tablespoons chopped fresh cilantro

FOR THE DIPPING SAUCE
½ cup Yoshida's Original Gourmet Sauce

2 tablespoons cashew butter

½ teaspoon sriracha sauce

FOR THE BASIL FRIED RICE
3 tablespoons peanut oil, divided

2 eggs beaten with a pinch of salt

1 clove garlic, peeled and crushed

½-inch piece of fresh ginger, peeled

1 dried red chile

1 medium onion, peeled and sliced

½ red bell pepper, seeded and cut into strips

½ green bell pepper, seeded and cut into strips

1 cup jasmine rice, cooked according to directions and cooled

10 basil leaves, stemmed and halved

¼ cup soy sauce

⅓ teaspoon sugar

Juices from rested beef

1 Combine the marinade ingredients in a small bowl. Place the steak in a gallon-size zip-top plastic bag and pour in the marinade. Marinate for 4 to 6 hours, refrigerated.

An hour before grilling, remove the bag from the refrigerator.

2 Set up your kamado for direct heat and preheat it to 500°F.

3 Stir the dipping sauce ingredients together in a small saucepan over medium-low heat on the stovetop for 5 to 8 minutes. Set aside.

4 Remove the steak from the marinade and pat dry. Grill to an internal temperature of 128°F for medium-rare, about 4 to 5 minutes per side. Transfer to a resting rack set over a pan to catch the juices.

5 Adjust the bottom vent to almost closed. Place a wok on the grill, close the dome lid, and allow the wok to preheat for 1 minute. Crack the dome lid slightly before opening it, to avoid flashback.

6 To make the fried rice, add 1 tablespoon peanut oil to the wok and swirl it around to coat the sides. Add the beaten egg and scramble it in the wok, then remove it to a plate and chop.

7 Wipe out the wok and add the remaining 2 tablespoons oil, garlic clove, ginger, and whole red chile. Allow the aromatics to season the oil for 20 to 30 seconds and then remove them from the oil.

8 Add the onion and bell peppers to the wok and stir-fire for 3 to 5 minutes, stirring frequently.

9 Add the cooked rice and stir until warmed through, 1 to 2 minutes. Add the basil, soy sauce, sugar, chopped egg, and any juices collected in the pan under the steak. Fold together and remove from the grill.

10 Cut the flank steak in thin slices against the grain. Serve with the fried rice and the dipping sauce.

WOK CARE

Treat your carbon-steel wok just like your cast-iron pots — clean only with hot water and a nylon brush. Dry over medium-low heat on the stovetop and then apply a thin coat of vegetable oil. Let sit over medium-low heat for 3 to 5 minutes and then shut off the stovetop and allow the wok to cool before storing.

#22
BRICK-PRESS GRILLING

Grilling chicken under foil-wrapped bricks sounds like a technique that started with the phrase, "Hold my beer and watch this...." But oddly enough, it actually comes from an old Tuscan recipe, *Pollo al Mattone*.

It might sound counterintuitive to press down on grilled chicken, since you always hear that you shouldn't press burgers or you'll squeeze the juices out. But applying pressure to whole cuts of meat actually helps them cook more evenly and yields crispy edges.

The technique is straightforward. Wrap a brick in aluminum foil and preheat it on the grill. Place the meat on the grill, lightly press the brick down on top of it, and let it cook that way. Because the meat has been pressed a bit thinner and has a hot brick on top, the meat will cook a little faster than it would otherwise. For chicken breast, it shaves about 1 minute off normal cooking times.

You can also use other things to serve as your press. Cast-iron bacon presses, cast-iron pans, griddles, or stoneware loaf pans are all good alternatives.

Brick-press grilling works well for spatchcocked chickens, Cornish hens, and butterflied chicken, as we're doing here. This recipe uses the technique three ways: for cooking the chicken, for toasting the bread, and for pressing the panini. You'll need two bricks, each wrapped in a 12 by 18-inch piece of aluminum foil, and a quarter sheet or other pan to hold the loaves.

BRICK-GRILLED CHICKEN PANINI

Serves: 4   Prep Time: 30 minutes, plus 4 hours brining   Grill Time: 15 minutes

3 boneless, skinless chicken breast halves, butterflied (see page 67)

2 quarts NMT Basic Brine (page 18)

4 teaspoons NMT Spicy Poultry Rub, divided (page 17)

1 onion, peeled and sliced

1 red bell pepper, seeded and cut into strips

1 green bell pepper, seeded and cut into strips

1 tablespoon canola oil

2 mini French bread loaves

2 tablespoons unsalted butter, melted

6 slices Baby Swiss cheese

6 slices provolone cheese

FOR THE SUN-DRIED TOMATO MAYONNAISE

½ cup mayonnaise

1 tablespoon finely minced sun-dried tomatoes

½ teaspoon dried oregano

¼ teaspoon garlic salt

1 Place the chicken in the brine and refrigerate for 4 to 6 hours.

2 To make the mayonnaise, in a small bowl, whisk together the mayonnaise, sun-dried tomato, oregano, and garlic salt. Cover and refrigerate for at least 1 hour prior to serving.

3 Set up your kamado for direct heat, place the wrapped bricks in the grill, and preheat it to 400°F.

4 Remove the chicken from the brine, rinse, and pat dry. Season with 1 tablespoon of the poultry rub.

5 Place the chicken on the grill and cover with the bricks. (You can top 2 side-by-side breasts with a single brick.) Grill for 4 minutes, remove the bricks and flip the chicken, replace the bricks, and grill another 4 minutes. Remove from the grill and keep warm by tenting with foil.

6 Toss the onion and peppers in a bowl with the 1 tablespoon oil and remaining 1 teaspoon poultry rub. Cook on the grill in a vegetable wok or on a griddle until tender, 6 to 8 minutes, stirring occasionally. Remove and set aside.

7 Split the mini French loaves in half lengthwise and brush the insides with the melted butter. Place cut side down on the grill grate and top with foil-covered bricks until the bread is toasted golden brown, 10 to 15 seconds.

8 Assemble the panini on a quarter sheet pan. Slice the chicken and divide between the 2 loaf bottoms. Top each with half the vegetables and then the cheese slices. Lightly spread the insides

of the loaf tops with the mayonnaise and press onto the bottoms.

9 Place the pan with the panini on the grill, top with the bricks, and press down to compress the sandwiches.

Shut the bottom vent, close the dome lid, and let the panini heat through, 3 to 4 minutes. Crack the dome lid before opening, to prevent flashback.

10 Cut the panini in half and serve.

TRY THIS NEXT!
Use the brick press grilling technique that I've described above to make GrillGrrrl's Rosemary Lemon Spatchcocked Chicken.
(grillgrrrl.com/2013/01/rosemary-lemon-spatchcocked-chicken)

#23
PLANK GRILLING

Wood-plank grilling is a form of indirect cooking that comes from the Pacific Northwest. Not only does it add a subtle smoke flavor, it makes a brilliant presentation when you serve it at the table on the plank. The kamado's tight air controls make it ideal for plank grilling, because you can keep the plank smoldering without much risk that it will actually catch fire — which can happen on open-air grills.

Planks used to be a little difficult to find. When you *could* find them, you had your choice of any type of wood — as long as

it was cedar. Now you can find grilling planks not only online but also in specialty stores and even grocery stores. You have more options than just cedar, such as alder, cherry, hickory, and sugar maple. You can save a good bit of coin by buying untreated wood shingles from a lumberyard.

To plank grill on a kamado, you first have to soak the planks for an hour. This isn't a matter of choice, like soaking wood chips — if you don't soak the planks, they *will* burn. Preheat the kamado to 350°F–375°F and place the soaked plank on the main cooking grate. Wait five minutes, place your food on the plank, and cook until it's done.

The classic plank grilled dish is salmon with "potlatch" seasoning and lemons, but just about any seafood works, including scallops, shrimp, and crabs. The shape and cooking time for pork tenderloins make them a prime candidate for plank grilling, too. You can even plank grill mashed potatoes on a kamado!

Ponzu-Glazed Salmon with Pineapple-Jalapeño Pico de Gallo

Serves: 4 to 6   Prep Time: 1 hour   Grill Time: 45 minutes

1 whole salmon fillet, 1½ to 2 pounds
½ teaspoon sea salt
½ teaspoon ground black pepper

For the Pineapple-Jalapeño Pico de Gallo

1 pineapple, cored and cut into slices
2 jalapeño chiles
1 red bell pepper
1 cup diced onion
¼ cup chopped fresh cilantro
2 tablespoons teriyaki sauce
½ teaspoon seasoned salt, or to taste

For the Ponzu Glaze

1 teaspoon vegetable oil
⅓ teaspoon minced garlic
½ tablespoon finely chopped fresh ginger
¼ cup ponzu sauce
¼ cup chicken or seafood stock
2 tablespoons light brown sugar
1½ teaspoons mirin (Japanese rice wine)
⅓ teaspoon finely chopped fresh cilantro
¼ teaspoon ground black pepper
½ teaspoon soy sauce
⅛ teaspoon Chinese five spice
1 tablespoon water
1 teaspoon cornstarch

1 Soak a wood grilling plank in water for 1 hour, weighing it down with a heavy pot to keep it submerged.

2. To make the pico de gallo, set up your kamado for direct heat and preheat it to 400°F. Grill the pineapple slices on

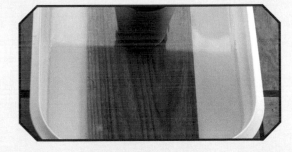

both sides, about 3 minutes per side. Char the jalapeños and bell pepper on the grill, about 5 to 7 minutes then place in a plastic bag to steam.

After 5 minutes, peel, seed, and dice them and place in a medium bowl. Cut the pineapple slices into bite-size chunks and add to the bowl. Stir in the diced onion, ¼ cup cilantro, teriyaki, and ½ teaspoon seasoned salt. Cover and refrigerate until ready to serve.

3 Close the bottom vent slightly to reduce the heat to 375°F.

4 For the ponzu glaze, heat the oil on the stovetop in a small saucepan over medium heat. Add the garlic and ginger and simmer for 30 seconds. Stir in the ponzu, stock, sugar, mirin, ⅓ teaspoon cilantro, black pepper, soy sauce, and five spice. Simmer for 5 minutes.

5 Whisk the water and cornstarch together in a small bowl to form a slurry. Stir into the glaze; simmer until thickened,

another 2 to 3 minutes. For a smooth texture, pulse in a blender, if you wish.

6 Remove the plank from the water, shake off the excess, and place it on the main cooking grate. Close the dome lid and wait 5 minutes.

7. Place the salmon on the plank, skin side down, and season with salt and pepper. Place on the grill, close the lid, and cook until the salmon reaches an internal temperature of 120°F, about 20 minutes.

8 Pour the glaze over the salmon and cook until the salmon reaches 130°F–140°F, about 5 more minutes.

Remove from the grill and serve with the pico de gallo.

#24

STEAM COOKING ON A KAMADO

This basic technique has been used around countless campfires as generations of Boy Scouts and Girl Scouts have cooked meals wrapped up in foil packets. It's a simple and effective method of steaming — but the idea of using a Bundt pan to steam crab legs on the grill just fell into my lap. Literally.

I was fixing crab legs and reached into a cabinet to get a cutting board when our Jenga stack of cake pans fell out of the cabinet. It struck me that the Bundt pan's unique shape was perfect. The natural bend of the crab legs makes them fit perfectly in layers around the pan. The curved pan bottom holds the legs up out of the steaming liquid. The center hole lets a little smoke flavor enter, while foil over the top keeps the steam in. It would be difficult to design something better for this purpose.

Beer-Steamed Snow Crab with Corn and Potatoes

Serves: 4   Prep Time: 15 minutes   Grill Time: 30 minutes

FOR THE CORN AND POTATOES
3 ears yellow corn, husks and silks removed, cut into thirds

1 lemon

1 pound Red Bliss potatoes, cut into 1-inch pieces

2 whole cloves garlic, peeled

¼ cup unsalted butter, cut into tablespoons

¼ cup beer

⅓ teaspoon kosher salt

2 tablespoons seafood seasoning

FOR THE SNOW CRAB
2 pounds snow crab clusters, thawed

1 lemon

2 tablespoons seafood seasoning

½ cup light beer, warmed

FOR SERVING
1 tablespoon chopped fresh parsley, for garnish

Clarified butter

||||||||||||||||||||||||||||||||||||||||||||||||||||||||||||||||||||||||||||||||||||||||||||

1   Set up your kamado for direct heat and preheat it to 350°F.

2   Cut both lemons in half (for the corn and potatoes and for the snow crab). Grill them cut side down until charred, 3 to 5 minutes.

3   Place an 18 x 18-inch sheet of heavy-duty aluminum foil on a work surface and top it with the corn, potatoes, garlic, and butter.

Drizzle with the juice of 2 charred lemon halves and ¼ cup beer. Season with the salt and the seafood seasoning. Throw on the squeezed lemon halves, too. Cover with a second piece of foil the same size and tightly fold all 4 sides to form a sealed packet. Place on the grill and grill with the lid closed. The total cooking time for this veggie pack will be about 25 to 30 minutes.

4   Meanwhile, season the snow crab clusters heavily with the seafood seasoning and place in a Bundt pan. Squeeze the juice from the remaining lemon halves into the warm beer; pour into the bottom of the Bundt pan. Add the squeezed lemon halves and tightly cover with a third sheet of foil.

7 To serve, drain off any liquid and then dump the crab and corn packages onto a table covered with banquet paper. Sprinkle with parsley and serve with clarified butter.

TRY THIS NEXT!

When grilling burgers, use the hobo-pack technique for sliced onions, adding a few pinches of salt and a pinch of sugar to make caramelized onions as a burger topper.

Try using your Bundt steamer to steam mussels over white wine and herbs.

5 When the corn pack has been on for 15 to 20 minutes, flip the pack and add the Bundt pan to the grill. Close the lid and cook until the crab is heated through, about 10 minutes.

6 Remove the packets from the grill. Open carefully, as the steam will be very hot. Use a fork to cut a vent for the steam to escape and then use heat/moisture-resistant gloves to open them.

#25
GRILL TOPPERS AND VEGGIE WOKS

Grill toppers are usually wire baskets or thin metal pans with holes, useful for cooking vegetables and other small foods on the grill. They prevent food from falling through the grate and keep you from having to individually turn pieces of food—you simply toss them in the pan. You may lose a stray vegetable or two through a hole, but that isn't a big deal. These pans are good for cooking veggies, small foods, and soft foods such as raw meatballs that would sink into the grill grates.

There are all types of grill toppers and vegetable woks, but you only need one to handle everything. Some have fixed components, while others have collapsible handles. Either type is generally inexpensive and durable; I've never had one break. There are even models that integrate into the grate itself, like the Craycort cast-iron veggie wok — convenient for cooking meat and veggies at the same time, like I did with this recipe.

Just like your grill grates, your toppers need to be kept clean and lubricated. Thin metal ones only take seconds to preheat.

Heavier units, such as cast iron, need to be preheated for at least five minutes.

My neighbor also has a kamado grill, and we often compare notes while we're outside cooking. One of his favorite weeknight meals from the kamado is fajita rice bowls made with grilled chicken thighs, onions, black beans, and corn. I thought I'd put my own spin on the dish by using beef and a cilantro and lime-flavored rice. To prepare this quickly at dinnertime, make the rice ahead of time and let the meat marinate while you're at work.

STEAK FAJITA RICE BOWLS

Serves: 4   Prep Time: 1 hour, plus 4 to 8 hours marinating   Grill Time: 15 minutes

1½-pound flank steak

1 onion, peeled and sliced

1 red bell pepper, seeded and cut into strips

1 green bell pepper, seeded and cut into strips

FOR THE MARINADE
½ cup vegetable oil

¼ cup lime juice

2 tablespoons canned diced green chiles

1 teaspoon garlic salt

1 teaspoon ground cumin

1 teaspoon chili powder

½ teaspoon dried oregano

¼ teaspoon ancho chile powder

FOR THE CILANTRO-LIME RICE
1 cup long-grain rice

1½ tablespoons lime juice

1 tablespoon unsalted butter, melted

½ teaspoon fajita seasoning

¼ cup chopped fresh cilantro

FOR THE FAJITA FINISHING SAUCE
2 tablespoons reserved marinade

¼ cup Mexican crema, sour cream, or plain Greek yogurt

1 tablespoon heavy cream

Pinch of kosher salt

Pinch of ground black pepper

FOR SERVING
4 corn tortilla bowls (optional)

1   In a bowl, stir together all the ingredients for the marinade. Reserve 2 tablespoons for the finishing sauce. Place the steak, onion, and peppers in a zip-top plastic bag and pour in the marinade. Seal and let marinate in the refrigerator for 4 to 6 hours.

2   Cook the rice according to the package directions. When done cooking and it's time to fluff the rice, mix in the lime juice, butter, fajita seasoning, and cilantro. Cover and keep warm while the steak grills. (If you're making the rice ahead of time, refrigerate and then reheat just before serving time.)

3   In a small bowl, whisk together all the ingredients for the finishing sauce. Set aside.

4   Set up your kamado for direct heat and preheat it to 450°F.

5   Remove the steak and veggies from the marinade and pat the steak dry.

6   If you are using an integrated wok, grill the steak and veggies at the same time.

Grill the steak until it hits an internal temperature of 128°F, about 4 to 5 minutes per side. Toss the peppers and onions with tongs every few minutes until softened and slightly charred in some places. Let the steak rest for 5 minutes prior to slicing.

If you are using a grill pan to cook the vegetables, first grill the steak on the grates until it hits an internal temperature of 128°F, about 4 to 5 minutes per side. Remove and let rest. Lightly oil the pan and place it on the grill. Add the veggies and cook, tossing occasionally, 6 to 8 minutes. Remove.

8 Using either soup bowls or the optional corn tortilla bowls, build each fajita bowl with ½ cup rice, grilled vegetables, sliced beef, and a drizzle of the finishing sauce.

TRY THIS NEXT!
Use a grill pan to cook your favorite meatballs and make a meatball sub for game day.

7. Thinly slice the steak across the grain.

#26

CORN THREE WAYS

There are a number of ways to grill corn on the cob. These three all start off the same, by soaking the corn in hot water for 45 minutes. That tempers and hydrates the corn, and in the case of husk-on corn, it also creates a steaming effect.

Husk On

1 Soak ears of corn, husks on, in hot tap water for 45 minutes.

2 Set up your kamado for direct heat and preheat it to 400°F.

3 Remove the corn from the water, shake off the excess, and place it on the main grate. Cover and cook for 20 to 25 minutes, turning every 3 to 5 minutes.

4 When the husks are charred, take the corn off the grill, remove the husks and silk, and serve.

Husk Off

When grilling corn this way, I like to actually keep the husks attached to the corn but pulled back and tied to create a fun handle. To keep the "handles" from burning, you can spend your hard-earned money on a fancy stainless steel skewer heat shield or you can just make your own by cutting an aluminum pan in half.

1   Peel the husks back and tie with kitchen twine. Remove the silks and soak the corn in hot tap water for 45 minutes.

2   Set up your kamado for direct heat and preheat it to 400°F.

3   Remove the corn from the water, shake off the excess, and place it on the main grate.

Cover and cook for 10 to 12 minutes, turning every 2 minutes. If you hear a kernel pop, it's time to turn again, even if the 2 minutes aren't up.

4   Brush with butter and season with sea salt during the last few minutes. When the corn is fragrant, the kernels are tender to the touch, and some of the kernels have charred, the corn is ready to take off the grill and serve.

BUTTER-BRAISED CORN

Our family's favorite way to cook corn is to butter-braise it on the grill. It's tender and buttery, and it stays warm while you grill your proteins.

Serves: 4   Prep Time: 55 minutes, including soaking   Grill Time: 25 minutes, including resting

4 ears corn, husks and silks removed
½ cup (1 stick) unsalted butter
1 tablespoon garlic salt

¼ teaspoon chili powder
¼ teaspoon dried parsley

1   Soak the corn in hot tap water for 45 minutes.

2   Set up your kamado for direct heat and preheat it to 400°F.

3   Place an 8 x 8-inch stoneware or other pan on the grate and add the butter, garlic salt, chili powder, and parsley.

4   Place the corn on the grill, close the lid, and cook for 8 minutes. Every 2 minutes, roll the ears in the melted butter and put back on the grill.

5   After 8 minutes, return the corn to the pan, remove from the grill, and cover tightly with aluminum foil.

Allow to rest for 15 minutes before serving.

#27
WOK-TOP "BROILING"

You often hear that if you can't grill a steak, you can broil it for a similar effect. But what happens when you need to mimic broiling on a kamado? Just "wok this way."

A wok lid is a fantastic way to redirect the heat from the fiery coals onto food. You aren't going to "broil" a steak on the grill, but there are times when you might want to apply top-down heat.

Case in point is the Kentucky Hot Brown, the famed sandwich from the Brown Hotel in Louisville. It's an open-faced sandwich of turkey, bacon, and tomato topped with a Mornay sauce browned under a broiler. After seeing short order cooks put lids over burgers on a griddle to melt the cheese, I realized the same trick might work with this sandwich on the grill.

Here is our grilled version that's a little spicy and has a Mexican twist. You might not find queso asadero labeled as such at your store, but look for something called "Mexican melting cheese." Cotija cheese is available in most U.S. grocery stores now, too. If you can't find these cheeses, you can always revert to the original and use Gruyère and Parmesan.

GRILLED KENTUCKY HOT BROWNS

Serves: 4   Prep Time: 30 minutes   Grill Time: 15 minutes

4 slices sourdough bread

2 tablespoons olive oil

12 slices bacon, cooked

1 pound cooked turkey breast, thinly sliced

2 medium tomatoes, sliced thin

FOR THE MORNAY SAUCE

1 cup whole milk

¼ teaspoon dried minced onion

2 tablespoons unsalted butter

2 tablespoons all-purpose flour

2 ounces queso asadero

1 tablespoon grated Cotija cheese

¼ teaspoon red pepper flakes

1   Set up your kamado for direct heat and preheat it to 450°F.

2   To make the Mornay sauce, heat the milk with the minced onion in a small saucepan over medium-low heat on the stovetop for 5 minutes, taking care to not let it reach a boil. In another pan, melt the butter over medium heat and whisk in the flour to make a blonde roux. While continuously whisking, slowly add the warm milk to the roux until well combined. Whisk in the cheeses and red pepper flakes. Set aside. If it cools and thickens before use, warm on the stovetop over low heat, and whisk in a tablespoon of heavy cream until you reach a sauce consistency.

3   Lightly brush one side of each bread slice with olive oil and toast on the grill for about 15 to 20 seconds. Remove. (Toast just one side—no, that's not a typo!)

4 Place 2 pieces of the bread, toasted side up, on a lightly greased quarter sheet pan. Top each one with 3 slices of bacon, 4 ounces of turkey, a few tomato slices, and a generous drizzle of Mornay sauce.

5 Place on the grill, cover with a wok top, and cook until the Mornay sauce is lightly bubbling and browning in spots, about 2 minutes.

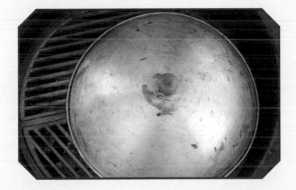

6 Repeat with the remaining 2 pieces of bread and the rest of the ingredients.

TRY THIS NEXT!

The next time you're grilling cheeseburgers, try using a wok top over them to get the cheese melted quickly.

#28
RAISED DIRECT GRILLING

Raised direct grilling is just what it says. It uses direct heat (page 27), but the cooking grate is elevated from its typical position on top of the fire ring.

Most kamado manufacturers and several other companies provide ways to configure a kamado to the raised direct position. Some use a grid extender to elevate a second grate above the main grate. Others use the heat deflector frame to elevate the main cooking grid. Still other companies offer multiple-level configurations, such as swing grates, adjustable rigs, and Woo rings. These are all viable ways to accomplish the same task.

But there are a few homemade setups that you can do for just a few dollars:

■ Simply raise the cooking grate four inches by positioning three fire bricks on their sides on top of the fire ring. Then set the cooking grate on top of the bricks.

- If you have a second cooking grate, you can put the first one on the fire ring as normal. Then place three empty cans of equal height at the 10, 2, and 6 o'clock positions and put the second grate on top of them.

- Buy a standard 18-inch grill grate, four (4-inch) bolts, four nuts, and eight washers to build your own raised grate as pictured.

There are three reasons that raised grids are frequently used. One is to increase capacity by using both the main grate and the raised one at the same time. Another is to get the food closer to the reflective dome heat in order to brown it more on top (as shown on page 133). A final reason is to achieve a sort of hybrid between direct and indirect cooking, using the raised grid to move the food away from the intense infrared heat of the coals but not blocking it completely. This last reason is why we use raised direct grilling for the following recipe: it makes it easier to get a savory golden crust while still cooking the chicken all the way through. A buttermilk marinade makes this grilled chicken tangy and tender.

GRILLED RANCH CHICKEN

Serves: 4 to 6   Prep Time: 30 minutes, plus 6 to 8 hours marinating   Grill Time: 40 minutes

1 whole chicken, cut into pieces

1 tablespoon chopped fresh cilantro, for garnish

FOR THE MARINADE
1½ cups buttermilk

½ cup plain nonfat Greek yogurt

2 tablespoons fresh chopped cilantro

1½ teaspoons kosher salt

1 tablespoon seasoned salt

1 tablespoon turbinado sugar

1 teaspoon dried minced garlic

1 teaspoon dried minced onion

1 teaspoon ground black pepper

½ teaspoon red pepper flakes

½ teaspoon dried lemon zest

½ cup canola oil

1 In a large bowl, combine all of the marinade ingredients except the oil. Slowly pour in the oil while whisking rapidly. Pour the marinade over the chicken and refrigerate, covered, for 6 to 8 hours.

2 Set up your kamado for raised direct cooking, using one of the options listed above, and preheat it to 375°F.

3 Remove the chicken from the marinade and set on a resting rack while the grill preheats to let the excess marinade drip off.

Place the pieces on the raised grate, close the lid, and cook for 25 to 30 minutes, flipping them every 5 minutes.

Remove from the grill as the breasts reach an internal temperature of 160°F and the dark meat pieces reach 175°F. Note that the pieces may not all be ready to come off at the same time.

4 Place on a platter, garnish with chopped cilantro, and serve family-style.

TRY THIS NEXT!

Utilize raised direct grilling to cook a Santa Maria–style beef tri-tip. Season the meat with garlic, salt, and pepper, and add oak chips to your lump coal (if possible, use oak lump coal as well). The classic Santa Maria uses a gear mechanism to raise and lower the meat while cooking over red oak coals. Use the raised grate for the slow roasting portion and sear directly on the regular cooking grate to mimic the effects of a Santa Maria grill.

#29
COOKING WITH STONEWARE

Their ceramic construction is a big part of what makes our kamado grills special, right? Using ceramic cookware on a kamado just makes sense, given that stoneware has a lot of the same properties as our grills. Stoneware is noncorrosive, so it won't rust as cast iron does; it's nonstick, once seasoned; and it's nonreactive, so it won't make acidic foods taste metallic. Like your kamado, stoneware has exemplary thermal characteristics that provide even cooking.

The two pieces of stoneware that I would recommend for someone wanting to get the most use out of a kamado grill are a quality pizza stone and a pie pan. The pizza stone can be used for pizzas, as a cookie sheet, and as a heat diffuser. The pie pan can serve as a drip pan, basting pan, baking pan, small saucepan, and hey—even a pie pan!

When using stoneware for baking, don't set it directly on a heat deflector or heat diffuser. Instead, use spacers of some sort to minimize conductive heat transferring to the stoneware. I use a set of stainless-steel pieces that I got at the hardware store for about a dollar. I lay them flat and set my cookware on them.

Using stoneware for "stovetop" functions such as sautéing, sauce-making, or simmering often requires that you open the grill lid frequently for stirring and adding ingredients. See Fire Management on page 4 to learn how to keep the temperature from skyrocketing while you're doing this. The ideal for this type of cooking is to start with your stoneware and grill preheated to 350°F. Lower than that is too cold, and much higher makes it difficult to control the fire with all the continuous opening.

Never, ever, *ever* add cold liquid to hot ceramics. If you do, you will likely hear a distinct "clink" and then the sound cartoons make when ice cracks underneath a character on a frozen lake.

Stoneware's thermal and nonstick properties make it ideal for this potsticker recipe. I guess they are technically "pot nonstickers," but you still get the golden bottom crust that potstickers have. You can either use one large stoneware casserole dish or do two batches in a stoneware pie pan. The horseradish sauce might seem a bit odd, but it gives it a bit of a wasabi taste without the heat. For the carrot purée I just smash leftover cooked carrot with a fork, but you could use very finely diced raw carrot and then simmer the dipping sauce a little longer, eight to ten minutes. Alternatively, you can just use carrot baby food, it's basically puréed carrots.

VEGGIE POTSTICKERS

Makes: 2 dozen   Prep Time: 30 minutes   Grill Time: 30 minutes

2 cups thinly sliced savoy cabbage

1 cup thinly sliced baby bok choy

½ jalapeño chile, seeded and diced

⅓ cup shredded carrot

2 tablespoons diced red bell pepper

¼ cup diced white onion

⅓ cup chopped unsalted, roasted peanuts

1 egg yolk

2 tablespoons horseradish sauce

1 tablespoon soy sauce

¼ cup water

1 tablespoon cornstarch

24 wonton wrappers

½ cup chicken stock

2 to 3 tablespoons unsalted butter

¼ cup very finely minced sweet onion

1 tablespoon very finely minced fresh ginger

1 tablespoon carrot purée

¼ cup chicken stock

¼ cup soy sauce

2 tablespoons unseasoned rice wine vinegar

||||||||||||||||||||||||||||||||||||||||||||||||||||||||||||||||||||||||||||||||||||||||||||||||||||||||||||||||||||

I   Make the dipping sauce by combining the ¼ cup minced onion, ginger, carrot purée, ¼ cup chicken stock, ¼ cup soy sauce, and rice wine vinegar in a small saucepan. Whisk to combine and bring to a simmer; let simmer over medium-low heat for 5 minutes and then remove from the stovetop to let cool.

2   In a bowl, mix together the cabbage, bok choy, jalapeño, shredded carrot, bell pepper, ¼ cup diced onion, and peanuts. In a separate small bowl, whisk together the egg yolk, horseradish sauce, and 1 tablespoon soy sauce. Stir the horseradish mixture into the cabbage mixture.

3   In a small bowl, stir together the water and cornstarch. Using a finger moistened with the mixture, lightly dampen the edges of a wonton wrapper. Place about 1 teaspoon cabbage mixture in the middle of the wrapper. Pull the wrapper corners together over the cabbage and then seal the edges by pressing them together. Repeat with the remaining wrappers.

4   Set up your kamado for direct heat, place a stoneware pie pan or casserole dish on the cooking grate, and preheat the grill to 350°F. Pour the chicken stock into a small, grill-safe saucepan and place in the grill with the lid closed while it preheats.

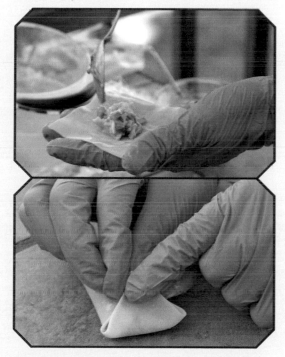

Melt the butter in the stoneware, using enough to thinly cover the entire bottom.

5 Working in batches, place the wontons in the stoneware pan, close the kamado lid, and cook for 2 minutes.

Lift the wontons with a spatula to make sure the bottoms are golden brown. If not, cook another minute or so until they are.

6 Add enough warm stock to cover the bottom of the pan or dish and tightly cover (with the casserole lid or foil). Close the kamado and cook for 4 more minutes.

7 Wearing heat-resistant gloves, remove the pan cover and cook until the moisture has evaporated, about 1 to 2 minutes. Serve the potstickers with the dipping sauce.

TRY THIS NEXT!

Try making "fusion" potstickers by using nontraditional filling ingredients. For example, we made Southwestern-style potstickers using leftover brisket, corn, black beans, chiles, and Southwest seasonings.

#30

USING GRILLGRATES

GrillGrates is the name of a specialty grilling surface that gives you sear marks worthy of a magazine photo shoot. Many competitive cooking teams started using GrillGrates when they came out a few years ago, and for the past three years the winners of the World Championship Steak Cookoff used them. For the backyard cook, GrillGrates provide more than impressive sear marks; the design also helps prevent flare-ups and makes handling delicate foods a breeze.

They are simple to use. Preheat the kamado to your desired cooking temperature; about five minutes before you're ready to cook, lay the GrillGrates on top of your normal cooking grate. Then just grill the way you normally would. There will be some steam and smoke as food cooks and juices vaporize when they hit the bottom of the grates. To get the classic crosshatch marks, rotate your food a quarter turn halfway through each side's cooking time.

You can also use the GrillGrates to create a reverse sear setup with the GrillGrates on the regular cooking grate and a raised grate above it. Roast the food on the raised grate, then remove it and sear the food directly on the GrillGrates. The advantage of this setup is that you don't have to remove hot ceramics to do the sear like some reverse sear setups.

The raised grid design has the side benefit of letting you lift delicate foods — like this sea bass — from below instead of trying to push a spatula underneath. Normally to flip the fish, you try to push a spatula between the fish and cooking grates and that force sometimes tears or breaks the fish. But with the GrillGrates, the lift tool goes between the raised rails, completely under the fish and then lifts straight up.

CHILEAN SEA BASS WITH PINEAPPLE-MANGO SALSA

Serves: 4   Prep Time: 20 minutes   Grill Time: 12 minutes

2 tablespoons unsalted butter, melted

2 teaspoons lemon juice

4 Chilean sea bass fillets, 6 to 7 ounces each

FOR THE PINEAPPLE-MANGO SALSA

1 cup diced pineapple

1 cup diced mango

1 jalapeño chile, seeded and diced

⅓ cup chopped fresh cilantro

2 tablespoons lime juice

½ cup diced red onion

½ teaspoon kosher salt

¼ teaspoon ground black pepper

FOR THE RUB

2 teaspoons Himalayan pink salt

½ teaspoon ancho chile powder

½ teaspoon garlic powder

½ teaspoon dried parsley

½ teaspoon dried lemon zest

¼ teaspoon ground coriander

¼ teaspoon ground annatto seed

|||||||||||||||||||||||||||||||||||||||||||||||||||||||||||||||||||||||||||||||||||||||||||||||||||||||||||||||||||||||

1   Mix all the salsa ingredients together in a bowl. Cover and refrigerate for at least 1 hour before serving.

2   Set up your kamado for direct heat and preheat it to 500°F. Once it's stabilized at that temperature, place the GrillGrates on the cooking grate.

3   Mix the melted butter and lemon juice together in a small container and brush onto both sides of the fish.

4   Combine the rub ingredients in a small bowl. Season the fish with the rub on both top and bottom.

5   Place the fillets on the GrillGrates and close the dome lid. Grill for 3 minutes, lift each fillet and rotate a quarter turn, and cook 3 more minutes. Flip the fillets over and repeat the process. When the internal temperature of the fish is 135°F–140°F, remove it from the grill.

6   Serve the grilled fish fillets with the pineapple-mango salsa on the side.

TRY THIS NEXT!

Use GrillGrates to make a Mexican-style pizza using tortillas for the crust and top with refried beans, cooked ground beef, salsa, cheese, and whatever other toppings you like.

#31

GRILLING
WITH SKEWERS

Whether you're cooking an appetizer or an entrée, skewers offer lots of possibilities for the kamado grill. Seemingly every country has its own version of a kebab, and there are almost as many types of skewers as there are recipes for skewered food. Metal, bamboo, sugar cane, herb stems, cocktail, round, flat, flexible — these are just some of your choices. Any of them will work, but stick (see what I did there?) to skewers a foot or less in length. The fancy long metal

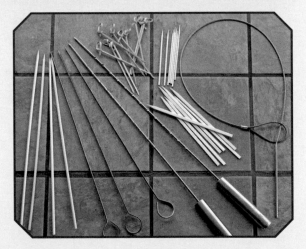

ones *will* fit into a regular kamado, but only across the middle, so only three or four of them can be accommodated.

When using wood skewers such as bamboo, it's important to soak them well first to slow them from burning. Problem is, wood floats. Submerge them in a glass of water and keep them down by stretching plastic wrap across the top.

You can buy a heat shield to protect the exposed part of your skewers, or try a home remedy. Wrap foil around the exposed base.

Or just snip off the excess parts.

You can make your own heat shield by cutting a foil pan in half.

Or you can skip all of that and use metal skewers. Be sure to get flat ones so your food won't slide around. There's nothing more frustrating than spinning a skewer and seeing that the food doesn't move at all.

PORK KEBABS WITH CASHEW SAUCE

Makes: 10 (6-inch) kebabs   Prep Time: 1 hour, plus 4 to 6 hours marinating   Grill Time: 30 minutes

1 pork tenderloin, trimmed of silver skin and cut into 1-inch cubes

FOR THE CASHEW SAUCE
⅓ cup sweetened coconut milk

¼ cup cashew butter

¼ cup beef stock

1 tablespoon coconut sugar (or white sugar)

1 teaspoon red curry paste

1 teaspoon soy sauce

⅓ teaspoon ground ginger

½ teaspoon fish sauce

1 clove garlic, finely minced

FOR THE MARINADE
½ cup cashew sauce

2 tablespoons unseasoned rice wine vinegar

2 tablespoons beef stock

¼ cup canola oil

1 Make the cashew sauce on your stovetop by combining all the ingredients in a saucepan over medium heat. Heat, stirring, until well blended, about 3 to 5 minutes.

2 Make the marinade by combining ½ cup of the cashew sauce with the rice wine vinegar, 2 tablespoons beef stock, and canola oil. Pour over the pork tenderloin cubes in a zip-top plastic bag, seal, and let marinate in the refrigerator for 4 to 6 hours. Cover and refrigerate the remaining cashew sauce.

3 Set up your kamado for direct heat and preheat it to 450°F. Warm the cashew sauce on the stovetop while preheating, whisking in another tablespoon or so of stock if needed for consistency and texture.

4 Thread the cubed pork onto 10 (6-inch) skewers. Place on the grill, close the lid, and grill until the kebabs reach an internal temperature of 145°F. This should take about 6 minutes on one side, then flip and grill another 6 minutes on the opposite side.

5 Remove from the grill and serve along with the warmed cashew sauce.

TRY THIS NEXT!
Double-skewer rows of shrimp, drizzle them with lemon butter, and sprinkle them with seafood seasoning. Grill over direct heat for 2 minutes a side at 500°F.

#32
FLEXIBLE SKEWERS

Skewers haven't really changed much in thousands of years — that is, until the recent arrival of flexible skewers. Flexible skewers typically consist of a length of metal cabling with a skewer on one end and a loop on the other. The benefit is easy handling during prep and on the grill. The down side is that you lose the fun and presentation of meat on a stick.

To use these, you treat the skewer end like a normal skewer and thread food onto it. But when it's full, you slide the food down onto the flexible part and repeat a few more times. Flexible skewers usually hold two or three times what regular skewers would. When the flexible section is loaded, you pass the skewer through the loop; now you can handle it by the one end, lowering the food into a marinade and lifting it out without getting your hands dirty.

Lay the skewer on the grill grate with the skewer end hanging out when the dome lid is closed. It will stay cool. When it's time to flip, you just open the dome, turn the skewer from one side to the other, and you're done way faster than you would be with a bunch of individual kebabs.

You can make these chicken kebabs with any type of skewer, but if you have a set of the flexible ones, use them for this recipe.

Curry Chicken
with Coconut Basil Rice

Serves: 4 to 6   Prep Time: 20 minutes, plus 4 hours for marinating   Grill Time: 45 minutes

2 boneless, skinless chicken breast halves, cut in 24 (1-inch) pieces

1½ bell peppers (mixed colors), cut into 24 (1-inch) pieces

For the Marinade
⅔ cup sweetened coconut milk

⅓ cup chicken stock

2 tablespoons chopped fresh cilantro

1 tablespoon red curry paste

2 teaspoons sriracha sauce

½ teaspoon kosher salt

For the Coconut Basil Rice
¾ cup coconut milk

1¼ cups chicken stock

1 clove garlic, minced

½ teaspoon kosher salt

¼ stalk fresh lemongrass

1 cup jasmine rice

2 tablespoons chopped fresh basil

½ teaspoon ground ginger

2 tablespoons sweetened coconut milk

||||||||||||||||||||||||||||||||||||||||||||||||||||||||||||||||||||||||||||||||||||||||||||||||||

I   Thread half the bell pepper and chicken pieces on a flexible skewer, alternating pepper and chicken.

Repeat on a second flexible skewer. Place both in a single gallon-size zip-top plastic bag, arranged so the straight ends stick out of the top.

2 Whisk the marinade ingredients together in a bowl and pour into the bag, working the marinade around the skewers. Place on a tray with a raised edge, resting the straight ends on the edge so the marinade won't leak out. Refrigerate for 4 hours.

3 Mix together the ¾ cup coconut milk, 1¼ cups chicken stock, garlic, ½ teaspoon salt, and lemongrass in a medium saucepan and bring to a boil on the stovetop over medium-high heat. Remove the lemongrass, add the jasmine rice, cover, lower the heat to a simmer, and cook for 25 minutes.

4 Rest the cooked rice, covered, for 5 minutes and then fluff in the basil, ginger, and 2 tablespoons coconut milk. Cover and keep warm.

5 Set up your kamado for direct heat and preheat it to 400°F.

6 Lift the skewers out of the marinade and shake off the excess. Lay them on the cooking grate, draping the straight ends out of the kamado. Close the grill and cook for 5 minutes.

7 Lift the straight ends and flip the skewers to the other side, again leaving the ends sticking out. Close and cook for 5 more minutes.

8 Check the internal temperature of the chicken, and if it has reached 165°F, pull the skewers from the grill. If not, flip back to the other side and cook for another 1 to 2 minutes, until done.

9 Place the cooked rice on a platter. Unhook the skewers and slide the grilled chicken and peppers onto the rice to serve family-style.

TRY THIS NEXT!
Use your favorite yakitori recipe with a set of flexible skewers. Grill and serve over seasoned noodles.

#33
SPIDER RIG SEARING

A Spider is a stainless-steel rig designed to fit on the fire ring of most standard-size kamado grills. Some kamado manufacturers offer similar products for their indirect setup, but these vary and may not have all of the functions described here.

A Spider can be used "legs up" with a 13-inch pizza stone to create an indirect setup (page 31). It can be used with the legs either up or down to hold a wok (page 91). Turn the legs down, put a cooking rack on top, and you have a setup for raised direct grilling (page 114).

Because it positions a grate just inches from the fiery coals for maximum heat, the Spider is useful for high-temp searing in conjunction with reverse sear (page 78), sous-vide (page 136), and sear roasting (page 75). To use it this way, put the Spider in the grill with the legs up and set a 13-inch cast-iron grate on it. Open the bottom and top vents all the way to bring the dome temperature above 500°F. The temperature near the coals will be intensely hot—hotter than 500°F—giving you searing power matching the special equipment used by steakhouses to sear their steaks.

Considering that intense heat and the use of flambé with this recipe, this is a good time to go back and review grilling safety. Heavy-duty fire-resistant gloves are a must, as these temperatures can melt silicone mitts in seconds. If things go wrong with the flambé, don't panic. Shut the dome lid and close down the vents to extinguish the fire.

Seared Beef Fillet with Creole Brandy Sauce

Serves: 4   Prep Time: 30 minutes   Grill Time: 1¼ hours

4 beef tenderloin fillets, 8 to 9 ounces each, trimmed and tied

4 teaspoons NMT Cajun Beef Rub (page 15) or NMT Beef Rub (page 15)

For the Creole Brandy Sauce
1 teaspoon salted butter

1 slice bacon, chopped

¼ cup finely diced mushrooms

1 tablespoon diced green onion, white portion only

¼ cup beef stock

2 tablespoons brandy, at least 80 proof

2 tablespoons Creole mustard

6 ounces heavy cream

1½ teaspoons smoked paprika

Kosher salt and ground black pepper to taste

1 Preheat your kamado to 300°F. Place the Spider on the fire ring, legs up, and top it with a 13-inch cast-iron grate for searing. Position a heat deflector and a standard grate above that for an indirect heat setup.

2 Season the fillets with the beef rub. Place the steaks on the top grate and close the lid.

3 Slow roast the steaks until they reach 5°F below your desired final internal temperature. It will take about 45 minutes to reach 128°F for medium-rare. (For more even cooking, flip the fillets when they reach 100°F.) Remove from the grill and tent with aluminum foil to keep warm.

4 Remove the cooking grate and heat deflector, leaving the Spider and cast-iron sear grate in place. Open the bottom and top vents to bring the temperature up to 500°F or higher.

5 Place the steaks on the sear grate and cook for 30 seconds, then rotate a quarter turn and sear for another 30 seconds. Flip and repeat on the other side. Remove and tent with foil to keep warm.

6 Put the cooking grate on the fire ring for a direct setup. Reduce the heat by closing the vent almost completely. Place a grill-safe skillet on the grate and preheat it for 1 minute.

7 Add butter to the skillet and sauté the bacon pieces for 2 minutes. Add the mushrooms and cook 2 more minutes. Add the onion and beef stock and cook until the liquid is almost all evaporated, about 1 minute.

8 Wearing protective gear and positioned safely by the kamado (*not* leaning over it), carefully pour the brandy into the

skillet and ignite using a long wand lighter or match. There will be an initial fireball, quickly reducing to almost invisible flames. Let this burn down until it goes out, about 20 to 30 seconds.

9 Stir in the mustard, cream, and paprika, whisking frequently, until the mixture thickens, 1 to 2 minutes. If it gets too hot and/or you see signs of the sauce "splitting," lift the pan off the grill but continue whisking, letting the pan heat finish the cooking. Add any collected juices from the resting steaks. Taste for seasoning and add several pinches of salt and pepper as needed.

10 To serve, ladle sauce onto 4 plates and top with the fillets.

TRY THIS NEXT!
Use the Spider setup for high-temp searing of tuna steaks on your kamado.

#34

PAN ROASTING

Pan roasting a split chicken is similar to cooking a spatchcocked chicken by the raised direct process (page 114), but it has an added benefit. Pan roasting retains the sucs (those tasty browned bits) and juices from the cooking proteins—which lets you make luscious and savory pan sauces. Use whatever seasonings you like to flavor a split and flattened chicken, then sear it in the pan and roast it according to the directions in the following recipe.

You'll need a good, heavy pan for this, so cast iron is a natural choice. A lidded 13-inch, double-handled cast-iron pan is an ideal fit for a standard-size kamado. You can use it for braising on the grill as well.

You can also finish a reverse-seared steak (page 78) by using the pan for the sear. Roast it with indirect heat as you normally would and then sear it in the pan over direct heat. To cut down on having to change the grill setup, you could even use the pan as your heat deflector so that it's already somewhat preheated. Then as the steak rests, sauté some onions and mushrooms in the pan, deglaze the pan with a few tablespoons of whiskey, and stir in some beef stock to create a delicious whiskey mushroom sauce.

SKILLET CHICKEN VERDE

Serves: 4 to 6   Prep Time: 20 minutes   Grill Time: 1 hour

1 whole chicken, spatchcocked
(Technique #5, page 36)
¾ cup salsa verde, divided (page 82)
1½ teaspoons kosher salt
1½ teaspoons garlic pepper seasoning

Oil for skillet
¼ cup white wine
¾ cup chicken stock
1 tablespoon cold unsalted butter

1   Set up your kamado for direct heat and preheat it to 375°F.

2   Prepare the salsa verde. If you use store bought sauce, increase the quantity to 1 cup. It is much thinner than homemade and you will need to reduce it. Reserve the ¼ cup of the salsa for the sauce and then simmer the remaining ¾ cup in a saucepan over medium heat on the stovetop for 10 to 15 minutes to thicken it.

3   Starting at the top of the chicken breast, work a finger between the skin and meat on one side. Push a spoonful or 2 of the salsa under the skin and massage it around to evenly cover the breast. Repeat for the other side of the breast and each thigh. Season the front and back of the chicken with the salt and garlic pepper seasoning.

4   Place a cast-iron skillet on the cooking grate and preheat it for 10 minutes. Use long tongs and a cloth to lightly wipe the pan with a high-heat oil.

5   Sear the chicken in the skillet, skin side down, for 5 minutes.

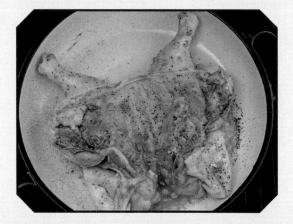

Flip the chicken skin side up and switch the skillet to a raised direct position (Technique #28, page 114). Close the dome and roast until the chicken reaches an internal temperature of 160°F in the breast and 175°F–180°F in the thighs, about 45 to 55 minutes. Transfer the chicken to a resting rack.

6 Deglaze the skillet by pouring in the wine and scraping the pan bottom with a wooden spoon to release the flavorful brown bits. Whisk in the chicken stock, ¼ cup salsa verde, and simmer until slightly reduced, about 5 minutes. You will know the sauce is done when you can drag a spoon across the pan and it will leave a clean streak for 1 to 2 seconds. Remove from heat and stir in the cold butter.

7 To serve, cut the chicken into pieces, arrange on a platter, and drizzle the skillet sauce over it.

TRY THIS NEXT!

Make Steak au Poivre using the skillet method combined with the sear/roast method. Find a Steak au Poivre recipe that you like and do the sear and pan sauce portions on the skillet. Remove the skillet and finish roasting the steaks with an indirect setup.

#35

SOUS-VIDE

Sous-vide is the ultimate geek technique when it comes to cooking. It used to be used primarily in commercial kitchens because the sous-vide machines were bulky and expensive. Then home-cooking enthusiasts started coming up with homemade solutions, like hacking a rice cooker or Crock-Pot, and they shared their ideas across the Internet. Now you can buy a unit made specifically for home use. Whether you make your own unit or buy one, you will also need a vacuum sealer for sous-vide.

The process involves seasoning food, vacuum-sealing it, and placing it in a warm, temperature-controlled bath to cook for anywhere from 2 to 48 hours. Then the food is quickly seared over high heat to add flavor and color. This is a more controlled version of the hot-tubbing trick (page 85).

Sous-vide promises juicy food and even cooking. So does the kamado grill. But sous-vide also provides the ability to precook and hold foods, which makes it especially useful for weeknights, or grilling for a group. The drawback is that even with the fire-seared finish, the grilled taste is less pronounced.

Sous-vide also allows food to be cooked below the standard 165°F. That's because the food stays long enough at a temperature that kills the germs and critters, not just momentarily as when it's cooked by standard methods. There are entire books devoted to this technique, and my intent here is simply to introduce the idea for those who might be interested in learning more.

With this recipe, I use the sous-vide machine not only to tenderly cook the chicken but also to keep the red jalapeño sauce warm after making it in advance. I use jarred red jalapeño except in late summer, when fresh red jalapeños are available. If using a fresh chile, you'll want to char, peel, and seed it first (see page 64).

Grilled Herb Chicken with Red Jalapeño Sauce

Serves: 4   Prep Time: 30 minutes   Grill Time: 6 minutes on the grill, plus 2 to 4 hours in the sous-vide

4 boneless, skinless chicken breast halves

2 teaspoons kosher salt

1 teaspoon ground black pepper

2 teaspoons chopped fresh thyme leaves

1 teaspoon granulated garlic

1 teaspoon chopped fresh rosemary

½ teaspoon chopped fresh sage

For the Red Jalapeño Sauce

4 tablespoons cold salted butter, divided

3 tablespoons all-purpose flour

2½ cups warm chicken stock

2 teaspoons finely diced red jalapeño chile

1 teaspoon chopped fresh parsley

¾ teaspoon kosher salt, or to taste

¼ teaspoon ground white pepper, or to taste

1   Preheat your sous-vide device to 146°F.

2   Mix the kosher salt, black pepper, thyme, garlic, rosemary, and sage together and season the chicken on both sides. Place in quart-size vacuum bags, vacuum out the air, and seal.

3   Place the sealed bags in the sous-vide device for 2 to 4 hours, following the manufacturer's instructions and making sure the bags are entirely submerged.

4   To make the jalapeño sauce, preheat a saucepan on the stovetop over medium heat. Melt 3 tablespoons of butter in the pan and stir in the flour until a blonde roux has formed, about 2 to 3 minutes.

5   Add the warm chicken stock, ¼ cup at a time, whisking until you have added all of it. Simmer over low heat until the sauce has thickened, being careful not to let it boil, about 15 minutes.

6   Add the jalapeño, parsley, ¾ teaspoon salt, and white pepper. Taste and add more salt and/or pepper if desired. Stir in the remaining tablespoon of butter.

7   Place the sauce in a zip-top plastic bag, force out the air, and seal (vacuum-sealing not required). You can do this up to a day in advance. An hour or 2 before you plan to serve, place in the sous-vide device, which is already at 146°F for the chicken.

8   Set up your kamado for direct heat and preheat it to 500°F.

9   When the chicken has been submerged for 2 to 4 hours, remove the bags from the water. Remove chicken from the bags and grill the pieces for 1 minute on each side.

10 Slice the chicken breasts and arrange on serving plates. Snip off one corner of the sauce bag and drizzle the sauce over the sliced chicken.

MORE ABOUT SOUS-VIDE

To learn more, check out Kenji Lopez-Alt's series on sous-vide cooking at SeriousEats.com.

#36
COLD SMOKING

Cold smoking is smoking at a low temperature to flavor food but not cook it. This technique is good for foods such as cheeses, raw nuts, and whole spices. There are a few ways to turn your kamado grill into a cold smoker. You can try to maintain a small fire using just a handful of coal beneath an ice-filled pie pan. You can buy a cold smoke generator that slowly burns wood chips or sawdust.

As far as I'm concerned, though, the easiest way is to make your own cold smoke generator using a new 25-watt soldering iron (around $15) and an unlined tin or steel can.

Simply drill 15 or so ⅛-inch holes in one side of the can. Drill a hole in the bottom of the can large enough to fit the metal base of the soldering iron (about ½ inch, depending on your iron). Remove the soldering tip and push the base of the iron into the can. Now fill the can with wood chips and cover the open end of the can with aluminum foil.

Clean out your kamado and place your smoke generator at the bottom, with the cord going out through the intake vent — opened just enough to let it pass through. Plug in the cord and close the grill lid, and you'll get about two hours of smoke with little to no heat.

For smoking cheese, you want the outdoor temperature to be 50°F or less so the cheese doesn't sweat.

Set up your smoke generator as described, and once you see puffs of smoke coming out, put blocks of whatever cheeses you like on the grates and close the grill. I like smoking Cheddar, Edam, Gouda, Colby Jack, pepper jack, and fontina cheeses with hickory chips, but try whatever cheeses and woods you prefer. There isn't any right or wrong here. Smoke for 1 hour for a mild smoke flavor, 1½ hours for medium, or 2 hours or more for a heavy dose of smoke.

Aging the cheese after smoking it is important to let the flavors balance. Vacuum-seal the blocks and refrigerate for at least two weeks before using. Then use your aged cheese in burgers, shredded on tacos, and melted in cheese sauces for a smoky kick. I think you'll never be satisfied with "smoked" cheese from the store ever again. Here's one of my favorite ways to use home-smoked cheese.

Smoked Fontina Cheese Mashed Potatoes

Serves: 8 to 10   Prep Time: 20 minutes   Grill Time: 45 minutes

2 pounds Red Bliss potatoes, peeled and cut into 1-inch pieces

3 cloves garlic, peeled

4 tablespoons (½ stick) unsalted butter, softened

½ teaspoon kosher salt

½ teaspoon ground black pepper

1¼ cups shredded smoked fontina cheese, divided

⅓ cup half and half

1 Preheat the kamado to 400°F and then set up for indirect cooking.

2 On your stovetop, boil the potatoes in a large pot of water until tender, about 12 to 15 minutes. During the last 1 or 2 minutes, add the whole peeled garlic cloves. Drain. Finely chop the garlic.

3 Place the potatoes, chopped garlic, and butter in a mixing bowl and mash together. Use a fork or masher for chunky, rustic-style mashed potatoes, or use a ricer or electric mixer for a smoother texture.

5 Stir in the salt, pepper, 1 cup of the cheese and all the half and half. Place in a greased 2-quart casserole dish. Top with the remaining cheese.

6 Fire-roast the mashed potatoes in the grill until they are heated through and the peaks are starting to turn golden brown, about 20 minutes.

Try This Next!

Try cold-smoking whole black peppercorns uncovered in a single layer on a tray or in a large bowl for 2 hours. Store in an airtight container for 2 weeks and then grind to use whenever you want a peppery, smoky kick in a beef dish.

#37

SALT-BLOCK GRILLING

Salt-block grilling is a form of indirect cooking in which food is cooked on a thick slab of Himalayan pink salt. Such salt blocks have been trendy in BBQ forums and at kamado festivals.

The slab gets hot and cooks steaks, chops, and fillets with conductive heat, and the smooth surface provides an even sear similar to what you get on a griddle. The slabs can even be preheated to 500°F for tabletop searing of thin strips of meat, fish, or vegetables. Salt blocks are seasonably available at specialty cooking stores and

higher end grocery stores or you can order them online all year. Shop around for pricing because I have seen a block selling at a grocery store for almost double the price of the same sized block selling at a specialty store.

Salt blocks require long, gentle preheating, so you need to plan ahead and be patient. Follow the supplier's preheating instructions, or you could crack your block and just have a bunch of salt. Count on at least 1½ hours to get the temperature to 500°F. If you don't want to spend that long adjusting your kamado from 200°F–500°F in increments, you can do the preheat in the oven and then carefully transfer the block to a kamado that's been set up for direct heat and is running at 500°F. The block will be hot enough to melt silicone, so use welder's gloves and metal tools to handle it.

If you put your food on dry, it won't absorb much saltiness. If your food is wet from a marinade or a thin coat of oil, it will draw out more salt. Take that into consideration and use low-sodium or salt-free seasonings.

The salt block will develop a patina with use over time. Follow the supplier's instructions for cleaning, but many grillers just carefully flip the stone after cooking to burn off any gunk. Then they cook on the other side next time. Alternating in that way will help prevent any nefarious buildup.

Grilling this tuna on a salt block imparts a mild saltiness that isn't overwhelming. If you cook the tuna on something other than a salt block, add a few pinches of sea salt to each steak. For the BBQ vinaigrette recipe on page 144, just visit the barbecue section of your grocery store and pick out something "islandy." The one we chose was "pineapple coconut mango tequila sauce." You'll notice there are no exact measurements for the tuna seasoning. We call this "6-pinch tuna" — you'll see why.

Salt-Seared Tuna Salad with Tropical BBQ Vinaigrette

Serves: 4   Prep Time: 30 minutes   Grill Time: 5 to 6 minutes

2 tuna steaks, 1 inch thick

Sea salt

Ground black pepper

Granulated garlic

Dried lemon peel

Ground ginger

Dried parsley

For the Salad

5 to 6 ounces spring mix salad greens

⅓ red onion, thinly sliced

2 blood oranges, peeled, sliced, and cut into 1-inch chunks

½ cup crispy chow mein noodles

For the Tropical BBQ Vinaigrette

¼ cup prepared tropical barbecue sauce

2 tablespoons lime juice

¼ teaspoon kosher salt

⅛ teaspoon ground ginger

1 clove garlic, minced

Juice from the butt ends of the blood oranges (about 1 to 2 tablespoons)

½ cup olive oil

1   Preheat an 8 x 8-inch or similar-sized Himalayan pink salt block to 500°F in the oven or on the grill, following the supplier's directions. If you want extra crispy chow mein noodles, toast them for 1 minute on the salt block when it is almost ready.

2   To make the vinaigrette, combine the BBQ sauce, lime juice, ¼ teaspoon salt, ⅛ teaspoon ginger, minced garlic, and orange juice in a small bowl. Slowly pour in the olive oil, whisking vigorously until well combined.

3   If you've preheated your salt stone on the grill, skip to Step 4. Otherwise, set up your kamado for direct heat and preheat it to 500°F. Carefully transfer the hot salt block to the main cooking grate.

4   Pat the tuna steaks dry and season each side with a pinch of pepper, a pinch of garlic, a pinch of dried lemon peel, a pinch of ginger, and a pinch of dried parsley.

5   Place the tuna steaks directly on the salt block, close the lid, and cook for 2½ minutes per side for medium-rare and 3 minutes per side for medium.

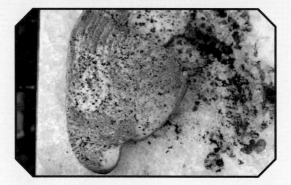

Remove to serve right away — there's no need to rest the fish.

6   To serve, divide the salad greens between 2 chilled plates. Top with red onion, blood orange pieces, and chow mein noodles. Slice the tuna steaks and sneak a small taste to check the seasoning from the salt block. Add a pinch of salt if needed and place on the salad. Drizzle with the tropical BBQ vinaigrette.

TRY THIS NEXT!

Give tabletop or bartop searing a shot. Sear thin strips of flank steak on a heated salt block to serve as an appetizer along with a ginger dipping sauce.

#38

SMOKING WITH ELECTRONIC CONTROLLERS

Electronic controllers for BBQ pits have been around for a while now, providing "set it and forget it" convenience. The typical setup consists of a proportional-integral-derivative (PID) control unit, one or more temperature probes, a blower, and an adapter to fit your particular BBQ pit. Basically, the control unit reads the temperature from the probe inside the smoker and tells the fan to blow in air as needed to raise the temperature.

Electronic controllers have become much more popular as new models have brought the price down under the $200 mark. The base models provide the basic function as described above, and that's it. The more expensive models add a wide array of features—Wi-Fi connectivity, multiple probes, open lid detection, ramp-down processes, and data logging capability by which you can control and record your cook from your laptop or wireless device.

The single most important piece of advice I can give if you're considering a controller is to learn to use your kamado with the manual vents first. A controller is *not* a magic bullet that will fix bad fire-management practices. For example, if you dump coal from the bottom of a bag onto used coal and ashes, your fire is likely to choke out — regardless of whether you're using vents or an electronic controller. If you set the controller to 450°F but have the top vent nearly closed, it's never going to hit 450°F no matter how much that fan blows. You still have to understand the basics of fire management.

Here are a few tips for using a controller:

- Read and understand the user guide. I know that isn't any fun, but you'll get more out of your unit from the start.

- Clean out the ashes before starting. A blocked vent is a blocked vent. And while the fans are low velocity, ashes by the vent can get blown around and land on your food. Likewise, clear away any dust and ashes around the fan's intake.

- Build a good fire and stabilize the kamado temperature before you hook up the controller and fan.

- Clip the temperature probe to the grate near where the food will be cooked. Make sure it's not over a hot spot — above heat deflector openings, for instance — as this could create false higher temperature readings.

- There will likely be a difference in what your controller reads for an internal temperature and what the thermometer on your kamado dome reads. Assuming the probe is correctly placed, this is due to the difference in heat between the grate level and the level of the dome thermometer.

- Keep the lid closed as much as possible. Every time it opens, the unit thinks the temperature has dropped 100°F because all of the hot air has rushed out. I use a unit without open lid detection, so I unplug it temporarily while the lid is open and then let the temperature recover for a minute or two before plugging it back in.

- Be patient. It's not a microwave, and temperatures don't turn around on a dime.

Some folks swear by these devices and the convenience they offer, while other folks look down on them because "they aren't traditional." I don't think there's anything wrong with using controllers. I just haven't used them a lot because they take the fun away from the kid in me who likes fiddling with fires. But I do like having that extra set of "eyes" on the smoker when I'm busy doing other things. Like most things to do with BBQ, it's a matter of personal preference.

If you do get an electronic controller, I recommend that your first cook be a shorter smoke rather than an overnighter.

Something like these delicious pork back ribs would be perfect. And while competitive BBQ cooks and judges may declare that "fall-off-the-bone" ribs are overcooked, cook them that way if that's what you like. Just increase the time in the foil (Step 5) by 15 to 30 minutes and decrease the time finishing the ribs (Step 6). I promise that I won't tell. Of course, you can also make these ribs without using a controller...

Baby Back Ribs with Bootlegger BBQ Sauce

Serves: 4 to 6   Prep Time: 15 minutes   Grill Time: 4 ½ hours

2 baby back pork ribs, membranes removed from rib backs

2 tablespoons yellow mustard (optional)

2 teaspoons ground black pepper

3 tablespoons NMT Basic BBQ Rub (page 14)

½ cup packed dark brown sugar, divided

¼ cup squeezable buttery spread

¼ cup agave nectar or honey (optional)

For the Bootlegger BBQ Sauce

⅓ cup ketchup

¼ cup Sweet Baby Ray's BBQ sauce

½ cup apple jelly

¼ cup apple pie–flavored moonshine*

¼ cup packed dark brown sugar

1 tablespoon hot sauce

1½ teaspoons Worcestershire sauce

½ teaspoon dried minced garlic

½ teaspoon dried onion flakes

¼ teaspoon ground black pepper

¼ teaspoon roasted ground cumin, (roasted is preferable)

⅛ teaspoon ground coriander

¼ teaspoon liquid smoke

¼ teaspoon ancho chile powder

Smoked salt to taste (about ½ teaspoon)

*If you don't want to use the moonshine, you can substitute 3 tablespoons apple juice and 1 tablespoon apple cider vinegar.

How to Remove the Membrane
From Pork Back Ribs

Some folks advise starting at one end of the rib, using a paper towel to securely grab a corner of the membrane on the back of the ribs, and peeling it off that way. This works okay with spare ribs but for pork back (aka baby back) ribs, this is the easiest and quickest way that I have found.

1. Use a dull knife to separate the membrane from the back of the bones somewhere in the middle of the rack of ribs. Stick your finger in this small gap and wiggle it back and forth, up and down, until you reach the other side of the rack.

2. Now curl your finger to form a "hook," hold the rib down with your other hand, and simply lift the membrane right off of the rib in one piece.

1   Clean out the ashes from your kamado. Add new coal and 4 or 5 fist-sized wood chunks to the fire box; top with any coal left from previous cooks.

Preheat to 250°F, and set up the grill for indirect heat, then connect the electronic controller, set at 240°F.

2   Spread the mustard on both sides of the ribs. This is optional, but it serves as a binder for the rub and you won't

taste it in the end. Season both sides of the ribs with the 2 teaspoons black pepper and then the BBQ rub.

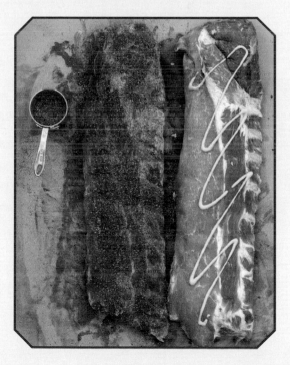

3 Once the smoke has changed to very light white or bluish, place the ribs on the main cooking grate, bone side down. Cover and cook for 2½ hours.

4 Meanwhile, make the bootlegger BBQ sauce. Put all the sauce ingredients in a medium saucepan and simmer on the stovetop over medium-low heat for 15 minutes, stirring occasionally. Let cool and then use a blender to create a smooth texture.

5 Fold 2 (18 x 48-inch) pieces of heavy-duty aluminum foil in half to form 18 x 24-inch pieces.

Lay the sheets on a work surface and sprinkle 2 tablespoons of the brown sugar down the middle of each sheet, followed by a squirt of squeezable spread the length of a rib.

Arrange a rib on the butter/sugar mixture, bone side up, and top with the rest of the brown sugar and more spread. If you like really sweet ribs, you can add a squirt of agave or honey on each side as well. Roll up the foil edges to seal the packets. Return the ribs to the kamado, bone side up; cover the grill and cook for 1 hour more.

6 Remove the foil packets from the grill and carefully open, watching for escaping hot steam. Remove the ribs from the foil, reserving ¼ cup of the liquid, and return them to the grill, bone side down, and close the lid. Cook until tender, about 30 to 60 minutes more. When the ribs bend easily when lifted at one end, they are ready to be sauced.

7 In a small bowl, stir together 1 cup of the BBQ sauce and the ¼ cup reserved juices. Brush onto both sides of the ribs and return to the grill for another 15 minutes. Remove from the grill and serve with the remaining sauce on the side.

TRY THIS NEXT!

Now that you're comfortable with using a controller, try an "over-nighter"—maybe a low-and-slow pork shoulder or beef brisket.

#39

Breakfast on the Kamado

Why make breakfast on the kamado? Well, why not?

Grilling breakfast might sound a bit unorthodox, but it's not that crazy if you've been up smoking BBQ all night and have a grill already going! There are flat-top grills built to fit into a kamado grill, and these are quite useful for whipping up breakfast. But a standard griddle plate or cast-iron pan works, too.

A plain breakfast "fatty" is a classic BBQ breakfast item and makes a good accompaniment to this French toast. A basic one is a pound of bulk breakfast sausage, seasoned with BBQ rub and smoked for about 1½ hours until it reaches an internal temperature of 170°F. If you want something more challenging, roll the uncooked sausage out flat, top it with cooked scrambled eggs, grated cheese, and sautéed vegetables, and then roll it back up and smoke the whole thing. Not enough? Okay, wrap all that in a bacon weave.

If making a fatty to go with this French toast, make the fatty first and then switch the kamado to direct heat by removing the heat deflector to cook the French toast.

This French toast has a secret. No, not that it was made with Italian bread. The secret is the sweet and creamy filling. Don't worry if a little filling sneaks out of one or two of the pieces — there will still be some left inside.

GRILLED STUFFED FRENCH TOAST

Serves: 4   Prep Time: 20 minutes   Grill Time: 15 minutes

1 loaf unsliced Italian bread

4 ounces cream cheese, softened

4 ounces mascarpone cheese

3 tablespoons confectioner's sugar, plus more for serving

⅓ cup seedless black raspberry jam

2 to 3 tablespoons butter for the griddle

Warm syrup, for serving

FOR THE CUSTARD

6 eggs

¼ cup whole milk

½ teaspoon vanilla extract

½ teaspoon ground cinnamon

¼ teaspoon kosher salt

1 Set up your kamado grill for direct heat and preheat it to 375°F. Place a flat-top grill, griddle plate, or cast-iron skillet in the grill once the heat has stabilized at 375°F.

2 In a bowl, whisk together the custard ingredients until they are well blended.

3 In another bowl, stir together the cream cheese, mascarpone cheese, and 3 tablespoons confectioner's sugar. Slice the bread loaf lengthwise through the middle, but don't cut it all the way apart. Open the cut loaf, like the pages of a book, and spread the cheese mixture on both halves. Top with the jam.

6 Dip half the slices in the custard mixture and place on the griddle. Cook until the bottom side is crispy and golden, about 45 seconds. Flip and cook the other side the same way. Remove to a resting rack and repeat with the rest of the bread slices.

4 Oil the griddle with butter, about 2 to 3 tablespoons depending on the size of the griddle.

5 Close the loaf and slice it into 1½-inch pieces. Secure with toothpicks.

7 Serve with warm syrup and more confectioner's sugar and a side of the sliced fatty.

Classic Breakfast "Fatty"

Makes: 10 to 12 slices   Prep Time: 10 minutes   Grill Time: 90 minutes

1 pound bulk pork sausage   1 to 2 teaspoons NMT Basic BBQ Rub (page 14)

1 Preheat the kamado to 250°F and then set up for low-and-slow smoking.

2 Remove sausage from the package and season on all sides with the BBQ rub.

3 Smoke the sausage until it reaches an internal temperature of 170°F, about 90 minutes. Since the raw sausage is soft, it will try to sink into the grill grates until it becomes firm from cooking. Place a piece of foil, a "Frogmat" (a brand name mesh grill topper), or mesh pizza tray underneath the fatty to support it.

4 Remove and rest for 5 minutes. Slice and serve.

TRY THIS NEXT!

Make breakfast quesadillas on the griddle plate. Stuff flour tortillas with scrambled eggs, fire-roasted chiles, sautéed onions, cheese, and browned chorizo sausage. Cook on each side until heated through, the cheese is melted, and the tortilla is crispy and golden.

#40
DIP AND FLIP

Dip and flip is a technique that builds layers of flavor by shuffling food back and forth between grilling and basting in seasoned liquids.

When the food is in the basting pan, it's getting a brief respite from the direct heat. As the food goes back on direct heat, the basting liquid clinging to it ends up cooking onto the food. It's not just the sauce flavoring the food; the food actually seasons the sauce, too, with a subtle smokiness.

To accomplish this, you need the right pan. Something too big will take up too much grill space. A pan that's too small won't accommodate all of your food. You also want something with a heavy bottom, to keep from scorching the braising liquid. An 8 x 8-inch stoneware pan is a good choice.

Dip and flip is best for smaller cuts of meat cooked over high heat, such as boneless chicken thighs/legs, pork chops, shrimp, fish fillets, and beef medallions. The liquid can be sweet, savory, and/or spicy, depending on what you're cooking. If you're grilling pork chops, for example, diced apples, brown sugar, and bourbon would work. But if you're grilling fish for tacos, then dried chiles, lime juice, and cilantro might be on tap. Butter is often a key component, because it helps the sauce coat and cling to the food. Pick ingredients that complement or contrast the rub you're using. If you'd use the ingredients in a marinade, then they should work as a baste.

This grilled shrimp appetizer is quick to throw together but still utilizes the dip-and-flip technique. Technically, it should be called Scampi-Style Shrimp on a Stick, but that just doesn't sound as good. Who cares, when it tastes this great?

SHRIMP SCAMPI ON A STICK

Makes: 6 appetizer portions   Prep Time: 30 minutes   Grill Time: 15 minutes

12 medium to large shrimp, peeled and deveined

1 tablespoon unsalted butter, melted

1 teaspoon lemon juice

6 thin slices Italian bread

2 tablespoons olive oil

FOR THE RUB

1 teaspoon Himalayan pink salt

¼ teaspoon ground black pepper

¼ teaspoon dried lemon peel

⅛ teaspoon cayenne pepper

⅛ teaspoon dried parsley

FOR THE BASTE

6 tablespoons (⅓ stick) unsalted butter, divided

1 tablespoon chopped garlic

1 tablespoon diced green onion, white portion only

¼ cup white wine

1½ teaspoons chopped fresh flat-leaf parsley

Kosher salt and ground black pepper to taste

1   Set up your kamado for direct heat and preheat it to 450°F. Place a skillet or stoneware pan on the grill to preheat.

2   If using wood skewers, soak them for at least 20 minutes in a glass of water topped with plastic wrap to keep the skewers submerged.

Thread 2 shrimp onto each of 6 (6-inch) skewers. Mix together the 1 tablespoon butter and 1 teaspoon lemon in a small bowl and brush onto the shrimp. Mix the dry rub ingredients together in a small dish and use to season the shrimp on both sides.

3   Lightly brush the bread with the olive oil on both sides and toast on the grill until golden brown, about 10 to 15 seconds per side. Remove and set aside.

4   To make the basting mixture, melt 2 tablespoons of the butter in the hot skillet and sauté the garlic and onion in the melted butter for 1 minute. Pour in the wine and let it simmer off, about another minute. Add the remaining 4 tablespoons butter, parsley, and a pinch each of salt and pepper. Move the pan to the coolest spot on the grill.

5   Place the shrimp skewers on the grate and grill on one side for 1½ minutes. Transfer to the pan, same side down, and cook for 30 seconds in the basting liquid.

6   Flip the shrimp in the pan to coat the other side and then move the skewers back to the grate, raw side down. Grill for 1½ minutes. Move back to the pan, same side down, and cook until the shrimp are cooked through, about 30 seconds.

Remove the pan from the grill.

7   Top each piece of toast with a shrimp skewer and drizzle on some of the basting sauce.

TRY THIS NEXT!
Grill chicken legs using the dip-and-flip technique and a baste of melted butter, lemon juice, and Italian seasonings.

#41

THE KAMADO AS A BRICK OVEN

With its curved ceramic dome and burning wood coals, the kamado does a bang-up job doubling as a wood-fired brick oven. Whether you're making deep-dish, thick-crust, or thin-crust pizza, the kamado can turn out some of the best you've ever had.

The most common pizza setup is with the heat deflector in "legs down" position, spacers on top of that, and then your pizza stone — all preheated. The point of the spacers is to minimize the conductive heat rising from the deflector. Otherwise the bottom crust will burn before the rest of the pizza is done.

Another setup is with the heat deflector "legs up," a cooking grate placed on that, and the pizza stone on top. This moves the heat deflector away from the gasket level and lessens the chance of frying your kamado's gasket with the fierce heat.

Besides being flexible, fun, and extremely tasty, pizzas cooked on your kamado have an extra benefit. The high temperature is effective at keeping the inside of your kamado clean and free of the buildup that comes from lower-temp cooking. My neighbor cooks pizzas at least once a week, and he almost never has to do a "clean burn" with his kamado.

The higher up you can get your pizza, the better—the heat radiating downward will help cook your toppings and brown the cheese.

Temperatures depend on the type of pizza you are cooking, but 550°F–600°F is a good range for most kinds. If you're aiming for a Neapolitan-style pizza such as Margherita, the temperature should be in the 700°F–900°F range, with an extremely short cooking time.

This pizza is one of my family's all-time favorites. We were making pizzas one night when I saw a bunch of leftover ABTs (jalapeño poppers) in the fridge. It occurred to me that if I sliced them, they'd make a good pizza topping—like mini-pepperoni slices. Sometimes we buy pizza dough from a local pizza joint (most places will sell it to you for a few bucks), but usually we make our own dough. For this particular pizza, we add 1 heaping tablespoon of diced roasted jalapeño to the dough.

ABT Pizza

Makes: 1 (14-inch) pizza   Prep Time: 10 minutes for purchased dough, 1½ hours for homemade dough   Grill Time: 8 to 10 minutes

6 to 8 ABTs (page 186), sliced less than ¼ inch thick
Pizza dough
1 cup shredded fresh mozzarella cheese

FOR THE WHITE SAUCE
2 tablespoons unsalted butter
2 tablespoons all-purpose flour
1 cup half and half
2 ounces queso-style cheese, shredded or cubed
¼ teaspoon Italian seasoning
¼ teaspoon red pepper flakes

1   Light the coal. When the kamado reaches about 350°F–400°F, place the heat deflector in (legs down), spacers, and your pizza stone on top. Allow the temperature to rise and stabilize at 550°F.

2   To make the white sauce, melt the butter in a saucepan set over medium heat on the stovetop. Stir in the flour and whisk until it is combined in a roux. Add the half and half, ¼ cup at a time, whisking continuously until all of it is incorporated. Bring to a simmer and stir in the cheese, Italian seasoning, and red pepper flakes. Cook until thickened, stirring occasionally, about 5 minutes.

3   Roll out the pizza dough on parchment paper to a circle that is slightly smaller than your pizza stone, form the edges, and use a fork to poke holes over the surface of the dough. Slide the parchment paper and dough onto the pizza stone in the grill, close the dome, and prebake for 3 minutes.

4   Remove the pizza from the grill and top with the white sauce, sliced ABTs, and mozzarella cheese.

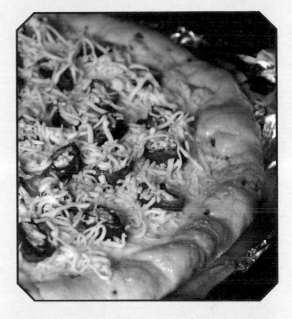

5   Return the pizza to the kamado and close the lid. Cook until the crust is golden and the cheese is bubbly and browning, about 6 to 8 minutes.

TRY THIS NEXT!

Busy weeknight? It's not the end of the world if you buy a premade "take and bake" pizza on the way home from work and throw it on your kamado.

#42
BAKING BREAD

The same design that makes the kamado a superb "brick" oven for pizzas also makes it the quintessential bread machine. The loaves come out with a thick, golden crust but are light and airy inside. Here are a few tips we've stumbled upon while learning to make bread on our kamados.

Clean yo' Kamado!

A clean grill is more important for baking bread than for any other type of cook. If you've been smoking or grilling a lot, you'll need to do a high-temperature "clean burn" (see page 9). You don't want your

bread smelling like pork butts and briskets. But more importantly, gunk that builds up inside your dome lid actually degrades its performance, because heat can't reflect off the dome as much. Make sure every inside air hole is free of blockages, and fill up your grill with fresh lump. You don't want anything messing up a rock-steady cooking temperature.

Setup

Preheat your kamado first and then set it up for convection baking (page 72) with the heat deflector "legs down." Use spacers between the deflector and your loaf pans. Speaking of loaf pans, use stoneware ones if at all possible. The dense ceramic material helps steady temperatures—just the way it does for the kamado. Stoneware does an exceptional job at converting the dough's surface into a flavorful crust.

No stand mixer?

No knead to skip bread-making. There are many recipes for no-knead bread, and lots of grillers have made these with good success.

We got this treasured recipe the old-fashioned way—someone shared it with us and showed us how to make it, hands on. Mary Alice is a fascinating woman who lives in our neighborhood. She carries herself with an elegance rarely seen these days. Before she retired, Mary Alice ran her family's 250-seat restaurant for 35 years, doling out family-style dishes such as chicken and dumplings. Her sourdough recipe was revered, and we are honored that she shared it with us for this book. You can use the same dough to make 10 mini loaves or 65 dinner rolls.

MARY ALICE'S SOURDOUGH BREAD

Makes: 2 or 3 loaves   Prep Time: 2 hours, plus 6 hours for the starter   Grill Time: 35 to 40 minutes

FOR THE SOURDOUGH STARTER
2 cups self-rising flour
½ cup sugar
2 packages rapid-rise yeast dissolved in 2 cups hot tap water

FOR THE BREAD
⅓ cup sugar (less if you prefer a less-sweet bread)
1 package rapid-rise yeast dissolved in 2 cups hot tap water
½ cup canola oil
2 cups sourdough starter
4½ to 5 cups bread flour, divided
Melted butter for brushing the bread tops

|||||||||||||||||||||||||||||||||||||||||||||||||||||||||||||||||||||||||||||||||||||||||||||||||||||

I   To make the sourdough starter, blend together the 2 cups self-rising flour and ½ cup sugar in a bowl. Stir in the yeast-water mixture, combining thoroughly.

Pour the starter into a glass container twice its size—it will grow in volume. Leave uncovered at room temperature for 6 hours.

2 Remove 2 cups of starter. Refrigerate the rest, covered, for up to 6 weeks (see sidebar).

3 For the bread dough, combine the ⅓ cup sugar and dissolved yeast mixture in a nonmetallic bowl. Stir in the canola oil and then the 2 cups starter. Add 4 cups bread flour and mix with a wooden spoon until the dough has a soft texture. You should use about 4 cups total, but go by texture.

4 Grease a nonmetallic bowl (roughly twice the volume of the dough), place the dough in the bowl, and set uncovered in a warm, draft-free area. Let rise until it reaches the top of the bowl, about 1 hour.

5 Spread ½ cup bread flour on a sheet of freezer paper or a silicone mat, then transfer the dough to the floured surface. Fold the dough over on itself by lifting the parchment or mat edges — no kneading required. Repeat several times.

6 Working on the floured surface, form the dough into 2 or 3 loaves, depending on the size of your pans. Place in greased pans and let rise again, about 45 minutes to 1 hour.

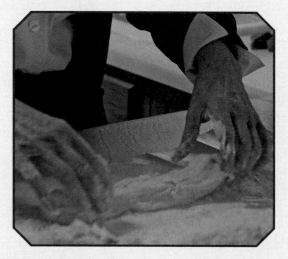

7 Preheat your kamado to 350°F. Once the temperature has stabilized, set up the grill for convection baking (page 72), with the heat deflector legs facing down.

8 Set the loaf pans on top of spacers on the heat deflector, close the lid, and bake until the crust is golden and the loaves make a hollow sound when you

tap them on the top, about 35 to 45 minutes. Halfway through that time, rotate the pans 180° for even cooking.

9 Brush the tops of the loaves with melted butter and remove to a resting rack to cool.

FEEDING THE STARTER

The next time you're ready to use the sourdough starter, take it out of the fridge and let it sit at room temperature for 2 hours. Dissolve 1 package of rapid-rise yeast in 2 cups of hot tap water. Then feed the starter by stirring in 2 cups of self-rising flour, ½ cup of sugar, and the dissolved yeast. Leave uncovered at room temperature for 6 hours and then proceed to Step 2.

#43
GRIDDLE COOKING

A griddle plate is a useful tool for getting the most out of your kamado. Griddles come in handy for cooking delicate foods such as trout or for creating an even, golden crust on steaks.

For standard-size kamados, a 16 x 9-inch cast-iron griddle plate will rest securely right on top of the fire ring. These are typically sold as "double burner" griddles because they're intended for stovetop use. One side is flat, while the reverse side is usually ridged to simulate grill marks. This type of griddle is going to be your most economical option and will last indefinitely if cared for.

Another option is a griddle plate insert like the one pictured to the left. This adds the ability to grill at the same time, but the trade-off is that you have less space. There are also some lavish enamel-coated griddle plates, but personally I think these are too costly and beautiful to go on a grill and get all smudged up.

Here are a few tips for getting started with griddle cooking on the kamado:

- Preheat the kamado and get the temperature stable, then add the griddle plate to let it preheat.

- Griddle cooking needs oil to be most effective. Add enough to coat the top but not much more, or you'll be dripping oil and starting grease flare-ups and smoke. You can also lightly oil your meat instead of the griddle.

- The ideal range for griddles on the kamado is 350°F–400°F. Below 300°F you won't get much browning. Between 300°F and 350°F you'll get browning, but it takes much longer to cook. Above 400°F you start running the risk of burning your oil, which doesn't taste good.

- Most griddle cooking requires frequent opening of the dome lid to check your food. While this is unavoidable, keep the dome lid closed as much as possible to keep the airflow and temperatures regulated.

This recipe originally was supposed to be "Tournedo Sliders," because a tournedo is just a filet mignon sliced in half horizontally. But spell check kept changing it to "Tornado Sliders" behind my back, so I improvised. Whatever you call them, sliders of crusty beef tenderloins topped with balsamic onions are just the ticket for Friday night happy hour. This recipe requires a lot of in and out of the kamado, but still keep the lid closed as much as possible to keep the temperatures stable.

SLIDERS MIGNON

Serves: 4   Prep Time: 20 minutes   Grill Time: 20 minutes

2 beef tenderloin fillets, 8 to 9 ounces each

2 teaspoons NMT Beef Rub (page 15)

2 to 3 tablespoons safflower or peanut oil

4 slider buns

1 large sweet onion, sliced into rings

Kosher salt and ground black pepper to taste

1½ tablespoons balsamic vinegar

4 to 8 slices Manchego cheese

1   Preheat your kamado to 375°F. Once the temperature has stabilized, add the griddle, flat side up, to preheat.

2   Cut the beef fillets in half, creating 4 ~~tournedos,~~ um....4 medallions. Season on both sides with the NMT Beef Rub.

3   Lightly oil the griddle, using just enough oil to cover. Toast the slider rolls on the griddle, insides facing down, for about 1 to 2 minutes. Remove and reserve.

4   Place the onions on the griddle, season with a pinch each of salt and pepper, and cook for 3 minutes. At first the onions will take up the entire griddle, but as they cook and become flexible, you can fit them to one side. Drizzle the balsamic vinegar over the onions.

5   Add the beef medallions to the griddle and cook for 3 minutes. Flip and cook for 3 more minutes for medium-rare. Taste an onion slice for doneness and seasoning; add salt and pepper if necessary. The onions should be ready to come off when the beef is done.

6   To assemble the sliders, place the medallions on the bun bottoms. Top with balsamic onions, cheese slices, and bun tops. Pour yourself a nice cold beverage and enjoy.

TRY THIS NEXT!
Make your favorite burrito and then finish it by searing it on a hot griddle plate.

#44

BLACKENING

Blackening is a cooking technique popularized by famed New Orleans chef Paul Prudhomme. Blackening *isn't* a euphemism for "burned." And putting blackening seasoning on a protein and grilling it, as many restaurants do, isn't blackening either. Blackening is cooking highly seasoned protein over extreme heat while basting it with butter to create a dark, spicy, and savory crust.

Many blackening recipes forewarn you about the amount of smoke this process makes, advising you to do it outdoors or to open up all your windows if you're blackening indoors. That makes the kamado an excellent option for this method.

Redfish fillets were the original blackened food, but the technique also works for steaks, chops, boneless chicken, and seafood. Use something heavy enough to handle the high heat, such as a griddle plate (page 166) or a cast-iron skillet (page 182). I did once put a Dutch oven lid upside down on a Spider rig (page 130) to use as a griddle for blackening steaks.

Remember the rule about not cooking above 400°F on a griddle? This is an exception. Your cooking temperature needs to be "rocket hot," 500°F or above. The short cooking time offsets the high temperature.

Be prepared for lots of smoke when the butter hits black iron. We're talking "I can't see, where did my food go?" amounts of smoke.

You also need to take extreme caution to not spill butter over the edge, or you *will* have flames in your kamado. As always, have your safety gear on. If you do get a flare-up while working in the cooking area, just shut the dome lid for a minute to snuff out the fire. Also keep the grill lid closed as much as possible to keep the temperatures regulated.

This technique is not for the timid griller, but the results are worth it. So strap on your safety gear and give it a shot. I recommend that you use long-handled tongs to remove the tenderloins and check their internal temperature, instead of trying to check it while standing over the super-hot fire.

Blackened Chicken Wraps

Serves: 4   Prep Time: 15 minutes   Grill Time: 20 minutes

8 chicken tenderloins, tendon removed

2 teaspoons NMT Blackening Seasoning, divided (page 16)

½ cup (1 stick) unsalted butter, melted

4 large flour tortillas

12 slices provolone cheese

2 cups spring mix salad greens

1 medium tomato, thinly sliced

½ red onion, thinly sliced

3 tablespoons prepared ranch dressing

1 Preheat your kamado grill to 500°F or higher. When the temperature has stabilized, add your griddle or cast-iron skillet and preheat it for 10 minutes.

2 Season the chicken on both sides with the blackening seasoning. Stir the remaining seasoning into the butter.

3 Place the tenderloins on the hot griddle and carefully ladle some of the seasoned butter over them. Cook for 2½ minutes.

4 Flip, baste with butter again, and cook for another 2½ minutes. Check the internal temperature. If it's 160°F or higher, remove the chicken from the grill. If not, baste again and cook until done, about 1 more minute.

5 Let the chicken rest for 5 minutes and then slice, on a bias, into ½-inch pieces.

6 Top each tortilla with 3 slices of cheese, salad greens, tomato, 2 of the sliced tenderloins, and onion. Drizzle with ranch dressing. For each tortilla, fold up one edge over the fillings, fold both sides in, and then roll up like a burrito. Slice in half to serve.

TRY THIS NEXT!

The next time you find yourself "stuck" with some thin ribeye steaks, give them the blackening treatment.

#45
SINGLE-SERVE DISHES

Ramekins and other single-serve bakeware haven't gotten enough love from the kamado community — yet.

We got the idea of using ramekins on the grill from steakhouses that serve sides in individual dishes. Any casserole-style side recipe is a candidate for cooking in ramekins. You can also use these dishes for main courses — think single-serve pot pies or baked ziti, for instance. Don't forget about dessert; you can bake single-serve cakes and soufflés on your kamado, too.

Your single-serve dishes need to be oven safe. Those made of glazed ceramic and cast iron are excellent choices. For main courses, use 1½-cup dishes. One-cup or smaller ramekins work for side dishes.

Indirect heat techniques are almost always used for cooking in these dishes. Don't place them directly on the heat deflector, because its conductive heat can burn the bottoms. Instead, use spacers to raise them up off the deflector. If you want significant browning on the tops, move the ramekins up closer to the dome lid. One way to do that is to turn a casserole dish upside down on the heat deflector and place your ramekins on top of it.

One advantage to using these dishes is that the ceramic or cast iron will keep the food warm for a while. So you can cook this Spinach Alexis, remove it to the kitchen to rest, and grill a couple of steaks. Your side dish will still be warm, ready to serve with the steaks.

One of Knoxville's well-known BBQ restaurants serves a cheese spinach dish called Spinach Maria that's "to die for." This is a spin on that dish that was created by my wife, Alexis.

SPINACH ALEXIS

Makes: 4 (1-cup) ramekins or 2 au gratin dishes   Prep Time: 30 minutes   Grill Time: 30 minutes

1½ cups half and half

½ teaspoon granulated garlic

½ teaspoon dry mustard powder

½ teaspoon red pepper flakes

3 tablespoons finely diced onion

1 tablespoon finely diced red bell pepper

3 tablespoons unsalted butter, divided

2 tablespoons all-purpose flour

½ cup shredded Velveeta Queso Blanco

½ cup shredded smoked Monterey Jack cheese, divided (page 139)

2 cups cooked, drained, and chopped spinach

¼ teaspoon smoked paprika

1   In a medium saucepan on the stovetop, heat the half and half, garlic, mustard, and pepper flakes to a low simmer over medium heat, being careful not to let it boil.

2   In a separate small saucepan over medium-high heat, sauté the onion and bell pepper in 1 tablespoon butter until softened, about 4 minutes. Leaving the onion and pepper in the pan, add the remaining butter and melt. Whisk in the flour and cook stirring occasionally, until it forms a light roux, about 2 minutes.

3   Whisk the roux mixture into the half and half, still over medium heat, and stir until combined.

4   Stir the queso and ¼ cup Monterey Jack cheese into the sauce; continue stirring until the cheese has melted. Stir in the spinach and remove from the heat.

5　Grease 4 (1-cup) ramekins (or 2 larger dishes) and pour the spinach mixture into them. Sprinkle the tops with the rest of the Monterey Jack cheese and the paprika.

6　Preheat your kamado to 350°F and set it up for convection baking (page 72), with the heat deflector legs facing down.

7　Place the ramekins on spacers on the heat deflector. Bake for 25 minutes, remove from the grill, and serve.

TRY THIS NEXT!
Spaghetti-and-meatball pot pie? Place your favorite spaghetti and meatballs in greased 1½-cup ramekins. Top with a crust made out of pizza dough, brushed with garlic butter. Bake in your kamado set up for convection baking at 350°F until the crust is golden.

"BECAUSE YOU CAN"

This isn't actually a technique for the kamado. It's more of a mindset to help you explore what your ceramic friend is capable of doing.

Some of the most creative dishes that I see in kamado and BBQ forums often are just to prove something can be done. Sometimes the result is a disaster and other times it might just be "meh." But you'll always learn something that you can apply in future cooks. Of course, you could just learn not to do that again, but that's valuable, right?

That's how this dish started. When I was thinking of ideas for this book, my wife suggested Shrimp and Grits. How in the world am I going to *grill* shrimp and grits? I discounted Alexis's suggestion, but by the next morning I was determined to figure out a way to do it.

This isn't your classic low-country shrimp and grits, but rather my take on a local restaurant's version. For the sausage, any tasso, andouille, or smoked, but not fully cooked, sausages work. I used a savarin

"BECAUSE YOU CAN" 175

mold with six individual ring cavities for my grit cakes, but you can also just pour the grits into a greased 8 x 8-inch pan and cut into six squares after chilling. Work delicately with the grit cakes when handling them. A thin fish spatula helps.

GRILLED SHRIMP AND GRITS APPETIZER

Serves: 6   Prep Time: 1 hour   Grill Time: 15 minutes

½ pound medium shrimp, peeled and deveined

1 cup yellow grits, prepared according to package directions

2 tablespoons unsalted butter, melted

FOR THE RUB

1 teaspoon pink salt or sea salt

¼ teaspoon dried thyme leaves

¼ teaspoon granulated garlic

⅛ teaspoon ground black pepper

⅛ teaspoon cayenne pepper

FOR THE SAUCE

1 tablespoon unsalted butter

¼ cup diced smoked sausage

¼ cup finely diced red bell pepper

1½ tablespoons all-purpose flour

1 cup seafood stock, warmed

1½ ounces Gouda cheese, shredded

½ teaspoon garlic salt

⅛ teaspoon cayenne pepper

Kosher salt and pepper to taste

I   Grease ring mold cavities or an 8 x 8-inch pan. Pour in the cooked grits and let cool, refrigerated, for 1 to 2 hours, until firm. Unmold, or cut into pieces if using a single pan; set aside.

2 In a small bowl, stir together all the ingredients for the seasoning rub. Set aside.

3 To make the sauce, melt the 1 tablespoon butter in a small saucepan over medium heat on the stovetop. Add the sausage and bell pepper and sauté for 3 minutes over medium-high heat. Stir in the flour to make a roux. Whisk in the warm stock and keep whisking until thoroughly combined. Add the cheese, garlic salt, and cayenne. Taste and adjust with kosher salt and/or ground black pepper as desired. Cover and keep warm over low heat.

4 Set up your kamado for direct heat and preheat it to 450°F.

5 Lightly brush the grit cakes with the 2 tablespoons melted butter and grill for 4 minutes on each side. Remove from the grill.

6 Thread the shrimp onto 6-inch skewers, 2 to a skewer, and lightly brush with the 2 tablespoons melted butter. Season

with the rub. Grill until done, about 2 minutes per side.

7 Slide the shrimp off the skewers. Top each grit cake with 2 shrimp and ladle some of the sauce over them.

JUST FOR GRINS

The next time you're stuck in traffic and bored, think of a dish that wouldn't be cooked on a kamado. Now spend the next 10 minutes figuring out how you would cook it on a kamado.

#47

ROULADE-STYLE ROASTS

If you really want to impress your guests with your grilling skills, knife work, and creativity, then roulade-style roasts are the way to go. "Roulade" is a French technique that literally means "roll it." You flatten out a piece of meat, stuff it with veggies, cheese, or whatever you choose, and then roll it back into a roast. When sliced for serving, the result is a dazzling presentation with stuffing swirled through each slice like a pinwheel.

My favorite cuts to use for roulades are flank steaks and pork loins. But you can

also apply this treatment to poultry breasts, boneless legs of lamb, and just about anything you can manage to get flat. You can ask your butcher to do it for you, but with a little practice you can do it yourself. A razor-sharp boning knife makes the job a lot easier.

Once the meat is flattened, the culinary imagination gets involved. The meat is your canvas, the stuffing your signature on this dish. Leaf vegetables such as spinach and Swiss chard work well and add bright color. For cheese, I prefer saltier, harder cheeses that don't melt easily — such as pecorino Romano, Parmesan, or Manchego — but you can use whatever you like. You can even stuff your meat with meat! Add cooked bacon or prosciutto to your stuffing if the mood strikes you. Lay your ingredients out on the meat, but leave a couple of inches at one edge without stuffing; this will be the flap that closes up the roast.

The hardest thing I had to learn about roulades was how to accurately measure the internal temperature of the meat. Was my probe in a piece of meat, or in the cheese mixture? I finally figured out to put a remote thermometer probe in the meat *before* rolling and tying it, inserting it in the edge that will be in the center of the roast.

When rolling up your roast, make sure that you roll with the meat's natural grain. That way you'll be cutting against the grain when you slice it into pinwheels. It helps to have another pair of hands hold the roulade while you tie. I like to start my first tie in the center, make the next two on the ends, and then fill in from there as necessary. A double overhand knot will keep the twine from slipping loose as you tie a second knot (like the first half of tying your shoes, except you pass the twine back under a second time).

One last thing about roulades. This is just my personal observation, but roulade-style roasts don't seem to rise in temperature during the rest after cooking as much as whole roasts do. So I cook them right to the lower range of the target internal temperature — for example, to 130°F for medium-rare (130°F–140°F range) — instead of pulling them 5° to 10° earlier. They cool off faster, too, so don't leave them waiting on the cutting board for too long. I prefer to serve them within a few minutes of when they come off the grill.

This is one of our favorite roulade recipes. It takes an unassuming $20 cut of beef and turns it into something that would rival a $100 beef tenderloin roast. You want a hefty flank steak, two pounds or more, to make the slicing easier.

Flank Steak Roulade with Manchego Cheese, Spinach, and Sun-Dried Tomatoes

Serves: 4 to 6   Prep Time: 30 minutes   Grill Time: 45 minutes

1 flank steak, 2 pounds or more

1½ cups lightly packed baby spinach, rinsed and drained

1½ ounces Manchego cheese, thinly sliced

¼ cup diced sun-dried tomatoes

2 teaspoons ground NMT Beef Rub (page 15), or your favorite beef seasoning

I   Place the flank steak on a firm cutting surface and apply light downward pressure with your non-cutting hand. Carefully slice the steak open horizontally along the longer side, spreading it out like a book as you cut.

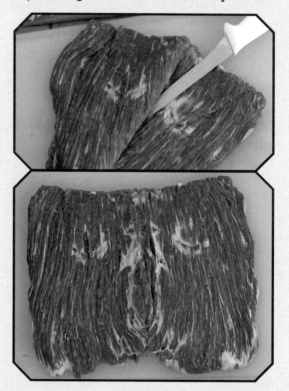

Stop cutting ½ inch from the other side. The meat should be mostly flat, but even out the thickness by pounding it with a meat mallet.

2   Cover the steak with the spinach, cheese slices, and sun-dried tomatoes, leaving 2 to 3 inches at one end uncovered. The uncovered end should be parallel to the grain of the meat to make the next step easier. Season with half of the rub.

3 Starting at the covered end, roll the roast toward the uncovered end, jelly-roll fashion. Tie with kitchen twine in 5 or 6 places.

4 Set up your kamado grill for direct heat and preheat it to 450°F–500°F.

5 Sear the roast on the grill with the lid closed for 2 minutes on each side. (Instead of lifting it up each time, you can just roll it across the grate.) Remove the seared meat from the grill.

6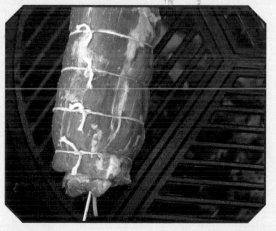

Switch the grill to indirect heat and close your lower vent partway to reduce the heat to 350°F–400°F. You don't have to wait for the temperature to get all the way down.

Place the roast back on the grill, close the lid, and cook until it reaches your desired finishing temperature, a little over 30 minutes for medium-rare.

7 Remove, slice, serve, and bask in adoration and praise from your guests.

TRY THIS NEXT!

Try spiral-slicing a pork loin roast. Slice as you would a flank steak, but make your cut ⅔ the depth of the roast; when you're close to the other edge and open the meat like a book, the part that's folded back will be twice as thick as the other side. Make another pass through the thick side, and when you're ½ inch from the edge, open it like a book, too. Or I guess with 3 folds, that makes it a pamphlet—but you get my drift.

#48
CAST-IRON SKILLETS

A good cast-iron skillet is a thing to be treasured for a lifetime and passed down through generations. It is also quite useful in the kamado.

Almost anything you can make on a griddle, you can cook in a cast-iron skillet on the grill. But you can't cook everything on a griddle that you can in a skillet. (The first examples that come to mind are skillet cornbread and pineapple upside-down cake.)

The main limiting factor with skillets is size — or more to the point, handle length.

My favorite cast-iron skillet handle is *exactly* ½ inch too long to fit into a normal-size kamado with the lid closed. Some kamado users have "handled" that literally by cutting off all or some of the handle with a cutting torch. You have to love the ingenuity of kamado owners. Of course, if that skillet was passed down through the family, that isn't an option, so don't even think about it.

If you've ever looked at my blog for more than a couple of minutes, you probably know that I'm about as close to being a vegetarian as I am to sprouting wings and flying. So what gives with a vegetarian burger? We just like these! Working with bean burgers can be a sticky situation, since they don't really hold their form until they cook. Two tricks for combating their clinginess: wear form-fitting food gloves (such as nitrile or latex) and use 5-inch wax paper squares to move the patties before cooking them.

Black Bean Burgers

Serves: 4   Prep Time: 15 minutes   Grill Time: 10 minutes

2 tablespoons canola oil

4 onion rolls

Lettuce

Tomato slices

Red onion slices

Alfalfa sprouts

For the Burger Patties

2 (15-ounce) cans black beans, rinsed and drained well

1 cup garbanzo beans, rinsed and drained well

2 tablespoons tahini paste

¼ cup chopped fresh cilantro

2 teaspoons diced, jarred red jalapeño chile

½ teaspoon kosher salt

¼ teaspoon seasoned salt

¼ teaspoon ground black pepper

¼ teaspoon ancho chile powder

2 cloves garlic, minced

2 egg yolks

1 to 2 tablespoons peanut oil or other high-temp oil

1   In a bowl, combine all the burger patty ingredients except for the egg yolks and oil. Coarsely mash using a fork or potato masher.

2   Put half the bean mixture into the bowl of a food processor along with the egg yolks; process into a paste. Return to the bowl with the other half of the bean mixture and mix with the fork or potato masher.

3   Divide the mixture into 4 portions and form into patties. An easy way to do this is to set a 4-inch mold on a 5-inch square of wax paper. Fill with 1 portion, turn upside down, and lift off the ring. Repeat 3 times. Chill the patties in the refrigerator for 30 minutes.

4 Set up your kamado grill for direct heat and preheat it to 375°F. Preheat a cast-iron skillet on the grate. Once preheated, lightly oil the skillet with the peanut oil.

5 Place the chilled patties in the skillet, close the dome lid, and grill for 4 to 5 minutes per side, being gentle when flipping them.

6 Place the grilled burger patties on the buns and top with lettuce, tomato, onion, and alfalfa sprouts. Serve with Sun-Dried Tomato Mayonnaise (page 96) or Avocado Ranch Dressing (page 89).

TRY THIS NEXT!

Make tequila steaks by marinating New York strip steaks in a mixture of tequila, olive oil, lime juice, garlic, and dried red chiles. Pan-sear the steaks in a cast-iron skillet over direct heat at 400°F.

#49
COORDINATING COOKS

One thing kamado cooks often run up against is trying to figure out how to cook several things at once when times and temperatures don't match up.

One strategy is to shift times. This is simple as long as the foods cook at the same temperature but for different times. Start Food A (takes 20 minutes) and then add Food B (takes 10 minutes) so that they both finish at the same time.

Another strategy we use is positioning. What happens when foods cook at different temperatures? If the difference isn't great and you're cooking with indirect heat, put the higher-temp food up on a raised grid and the lower-temp food on the main grid. If cooking direct, reverse that arrangement.

Sometimes you can adjust times and temps for a food, as we did for this mixed grill. The bacon-wrapped tater tots normally cook at 450°F for 20 minutes, while the "turtle eggs" and ABT (Atomic Buffalo Turds) cook at 250°F for 1½ hours. We lowered the temp and increased the time for the tater tots. For the other two, we increased the cooking temp and decreased the cooking time. So they all ended up cooking together at 350°F for 1 hour.

It doesn't always work out that perfectly, of course.

Are your friends coming over to watch the big game and expecting a smorgasbord? This trifecta of treats should satisfy them!

TURTLE EGGS

Makes: 12 turtle eggs   Prep Time: 20 minutes   Grill Time: 1 to 1½ hours, depending on grill temperature

1 pound bulk breakfast sausage
3 ounces cream cheese, softened
½ cup shredded cheese of your choice

1 heaping tablespoon finely diced jalapeño chile
1 teaspoon NMT Basic BBQ Rub, divided (page 14)

1 Slice the sausage into 12 patties and set aside.

2 In a medium bowl, mix together the cream cheese, shredded cheese, jalapeño, and ½ teaspoon BBQ rub.

3 Place a marble-size piece of the cheese mixture on each sausage patty. Bring the patty edges up to seal the sausage around the cheese. Season the outside with the remaining ½ teaspoon of BBQ rub.

4 Preheat your kamado to 350°F and set it up for indirect cooking. Place the stuffed sausage patties on the grill, close the lid, and cook for 1 hour. Or preheat to 250°F and cook for 1½ hours.

ABTs

Makes: 12 ABTs   Prep Time: 15 minutes   Grill Time: 1 to 1½ hours, depending on grill temperature

4 ounces cream cheese, softened
½ cup shredded cheese of your choice
1 teaspoon NMT Basic BBQ Rub, divided (page 14)

6 jalapeño chiles
6 slices bacon, cut in half

1. In a small bowl, mix together the cream cheese, shredded cheese, and ½ teaspoon of the BBQ rub.

2. Slice the jalapeños in half lengthwise and scrape out the seeds. Fill each half with some of the cheese mixture.

3. Wrap a piece of bacon around each stuffed jalapeño half; secure with a toothpick. Season with the remaining ½ teaspoon BBQ rub.

4. Set up your kamado for indirect heat and preheat it to 350°F. Place the stuffed peppers on the grill, close the lid, and cook for 1 hour. Or preheat to 250°F and cook for 1½ hours.

BACON-WRAPPED TOTS

Makes: 24 tots   Prep Time: 15 minutes   Grill Time: 20 minutes to 1 hour, depending on grill temperature

12 bacon slices, cut in half
24 frozen tater tots, partially thawed

1 tablespoon brown sugar
1½ teaspoons NMT Basic BBQ Rub (page 14)

1. Wrap a bacon piece around a partially thawed tater tot and secure with a toothpick. Repeat to make however many you want.

2. Sprinkle the bacon-wrapped tots with a little brown sugar and BBQ rub.

3. Set up your kamado for indirect heat and preheat it to 350°F. Place the tots on the grill, close the lid, and cook for 1 hour. Or preheat to 450°F and cook for 20 to 25 minutes.

Turtle Eggs

These smoked or grilled jalapeño- and cheese-stuffed sausage balls are based on the classic BBQ appetizer—Armadillo Eggs. Armadillo Eggs are sausage wrapped around a whole stuffed jalapeño chile, so they are spicy and too big for one or two bites. This is a smaller and milder version that I discovered with my friend and fellow kamado user, Jason Griffin (aka Griff's Grub on the web).

ABTs

These are easily the most popular BBQ appetizer on BBQ forums and at BBQ events. Traditionally they are a slow smoked, bacon wrapped, and cheese (and possibly cocktail wiener) stuffed jalapeño but there are many variations. Just don't call them a "jalapeño popper" or BBQ folks might look at you funny.

Bacon-Wrapped Tots

These are relatively new on the BBQ appetizer menu but they certainly get a response. Normally it is "Bacon-wrapped tater tots? That's ridiculous" followed up by "WOW, I have to make these!" once they taste one. Lowest common denominator food? Perhaps. But taste one…

#50
BEER-CAN CHICKEN

In general, beer-can chicken doesn't work as well on a kamado as it does on other grills. If you try to grill it with the heat deflector in place, that positions the breast (the fastest-cooking part) up in the hottest part of an indirect kamado and the legs/thighs (the slower-cooking parts) in the cooler part. Basically you have to flip the chicken upside down, and then all of your liquid pours out. Not my idea of fun.

I'm partially kidding here, but it is true that beer-can chicken is not an optimum method on a kamado. That's why most kamado grillers opt for the superior spatchcocked chicken (page 38), which cooks more evenly because it is all flat and close to the same position on the grill. That made me think that it was unfortunate that chickens weren't shorter.

Shorter chickens, you say? Cornish hens are the answer!

Shot Glass Cornish Hens

Serves: 2 to 4   Prep Time: 15 minutes   Grill Time: 45 minutes

2 Cornish hens, thawed

2 large cloves garlic, peeled and smashed

2 tablespoons beer (apply remainder to chef)

For the Rub

½ teaspoon kosher salt

½ teaspoon turbinado sugar

¼ teaspoon celery salt

¼ teaspoon dried oregano

¼ teaspoon ground black pepper

¼ teaspoon dried lemon peel

¼ teaspoon dried parsley

⅛ teaspoon red pepper flakes

For the Optional Glaze

2 tablespoons agave nectar

2 tablespoons unsalted butter

1   Preheat your kamado grill to 450°F and set it up for indirect heat.

2   Mix the rub ingredients together in a small bowl. Season the hens all over with the rub.

3   Split the beer between 2 shot glasses and drop a garlic clove into each glass.

Slide a shot glass into a hen's nether regions and place the hen on the cooking grate, using the shot glass and the hen's legs to form a supportive tripod. Repeat with the second hen.

4   Close the grill lid and cook the hens until the internal temperature registers 160°F for the breast and 175°F–180°F for the thighs, about 40 to 45 minutes.

5   While the hens cook, make the sweet glaze on the stovetop by mixing the agave and butter together in a small saucepan over medium heat.

6   Remove the hens from the grill, brush immediately while still hot with the glaze if using, and serve.

#51
GRILLING ON THE COALS

A caveman would probably be pretty impressed that we put fire in a container, place a rack over it, and then cook. But cooking directly *on* (not over) hot coals—as cavemen might have done—is equally impressive and has been regaining popularity. Barbecue expert/author Steven Raichlen has been a big proponent of grilling "in the embers" or "caveman-style" for years. Grilling innovator Adam Perry Lang calls the technique "clinching," and I recall the Food Network's Alton Brown

using this technique in an episode of *Good Eats*.

Most recipes using this technique call for a bed of hot coals. How does that translate to a kamado, since you don't have a specific temperature to go by? What has worked for me is starting with a smaller load of coal, filling the fire box only up to the air holes. I start the fire as normal and let the dome temperature come up to 350°F–400°F. At that point, I stir the hot coals once, close the lid again, and wait 10 minutes just to make sure the coals are evenly lit. Then just one more stir to knock off any loose ash or debris, and I've got a nice, compact bed of coals ready for grilling.

Usually this technique is used with beef. Steaks are a popular choice, placed directly in the glowing embers.

From personal experience, I know that putting $100 worth of meat or more into coals can be a little intimidating, so for this recipe I wanted to come up with a less risky version of grilling on the coals. Instead of setting the meat down in the coals, I brought the coals up to the meat. By spreading sticks of wood on the grate above the hot coals, you'll still get the burning embers and smoke flavor.

I got this idea from fellow user "Richard FL," in the Green Egg online forum. Not only was he kind enough to share the idea years ago, he actually mailed me the persimmon sticks from his yard! You can use sticks from hickory, oak, fruit trees — pretty much any wood. You'll need about a half pound (a heaping plateful) of pencil-size sticks. They need to be about an inch longer than the food you're cooking — so for these lamb chops, four to six inches.

Persimmon-Grilled Lamb Chops

Serves: 4   Prep Time: 15 minutes   Grill Time: 30 minutes

8 lamb loin chops

For the Glaze
½ cup apricot preserves
2 tablespoons beef stock
1½ teaspoons white wine vinegar

For the Rub
1 teaspoon kosher salt
½ teaspoon turbinado sugar
¼ teaspoon ground black pepper
¼ teaspoon dried lemon peel
¼ teaspoon dried mint
¼ teaspoon dried tarragon
¼ teaspoon dry mustard powder
¼ teaspoon ground cardamom

1   Set up your kamado for direct heat and preheat it to 400°F.

2   Combine the glaze ingredients in a small saucepan on the stovetop over low heat. Simmer for 5 minutes and

then let cool. If you prefer a smoother texture, process with an immersion blender.

3   Mix the rub ingredients together in a small bowl.

4   About 5 minutes before cooking, place sticks in a row across the grill grate (see note above). They should be perpendicular to the grate direction so they won't fall through.

5   Season the chops with the rub and place them directly on the sticks. The sticks probably won't be smoldering yet but will be close to it. Close the dome lid and cook until the lamb chops reach your desired internal temperature, flipping them every 5 minutes. (The sticks will start to burn and smolder — don't worry.) We like our lamb more done than most, so we cook these chops until they reach an internal temperature of 140°F, a little over 15 minutes.

6   Remove from the grill and immediately apply the apricot glaze. Let rest for 5 minutes and serve.

TRY THIS NEXT!

My favorite dish grilled this way is the Colombian specialty Lomo al Trapo. Try making it yourself!

If you follow Steven Raichlen's recipe from his book, *Planet Barbecue*, and rest a towel and salt-wrapped beef tenderloin in a bed of coals, your cooking time for medium should be about 9 minutes for the first side and 8 for the second.

#52

PRIME RIB

Prime rib is the king of roasts. The rich, beefy taste, tender texture, and luscious au jus are even better when cooked on the grill.

You have several choices to make that will determine what you buy at the store. First is the grade of beef. Just because it is "prime rib" doesn't mean it's graded as prime beef; the "prime" in "prime rib" refers to the primal rib from which it is cut. Choose beef that is graded USDA Prime or Choice.

Next is to choose either bone-in or boneless. Bone in is a more dramatic presentation when you bring it out to serve and you get to keep the beef ribs for yourself as the "chef's treat." If you get a bone-in roast, make sure to ask the butcher to slice off the bones and then retie them back with the roast. This will make it easier when it comes time to slice the roast. A boneless rib roast is easier to find. You can buy a 13- to 15-pound whole, boneless rib roast at warehouse clubs. Cut off the size roast that you need and you can slice the rest into ribeye steaks for later.

Finally, you need to know how much to buy for your guests. For bone-in roasts, assume a ¾-pound serving per person or count one rib bone for every two to three guests. For boneless roasts, use a ½-pound serving per person as your guide.

There are several ways to cook a prime rib on the kamado grill. The easiest would be to just fire-roast it by using an indirect setup (page 31) at 350°F for the entire time. That will work similarly to roasting it in an oven and you will have layers of doneness working toward the center of the roast; the outer edges will be well done, medium inside of that, and then a bit of medium-rare in the very center of the roast. You can also use the sear/roasting method (page 75) by starting with a high-temperature sear (500°F) and then slow roasting it at about 300°F until it reaches your desired internal temperature.

Those methods are good but my absolute favorite method for preparing a prime rib is to do a reverse sear cook (page 81) coupled with a roasting pan and rack setup (page 55) for making your au jus. This will give you that "wall-to-wall" medium-rare all the way through your roast. If your pan is the right size, you can actually forgo the usual indirect setup because the roasting pan can act as your heat deflector at a low cooking temperature. An 8 x 8-inch square stoneware baker is good for smaller roasts (5 to 6 pounds). A 13-inch stoneware casserole pan is good for cooking a whole rib roast (14 pounds) like we did here. Use the smallest pan that you can get away with because the more surface area that your beef stock has, the more it will evaporate during the cooking process.

So if the whole prime rib is cooked to medium-rare, what do you do for guests who prefer medium or medium-well? If you are cooking a large roast like this one, you can simply cut it into two or more roasts and stagger the times that you put them onto the grill by 15 to 20 minutes. This way they should all finish close to the same time but one would be around 145°F and the next one about 130–135°F. Just remember that this big roast will have 5 to 10 degrees of carryover cooking so you would need to pull it off of the grill before it hits your final target internal temperature. Generally, this will be about 15 to 20 minutes per pound, but go by your internal temperatures. If you have someone that just doesn't like to see red meat, you can put a medium-rare slice into a sauté pan of simmering beef stock for about 45 seconds to 1 minute per side.

Reverse Seared Prime Rib

Serves: 2 per pound   Prep Time: 45 minutes   Cooking Time: 3 to 5 hours

14-pound boneless beef rib roast

1 tablespoon water

1 tablespoon beef base

1 teaspoon Worcestershire sauce

2 to 3 tablespoons NMT Beef Rub (page 15)

3 to 4 cups beef stock (or enough to fill the pan to 1-inch deep)

2 cloves garlic, peeled and crushed

1 sprig fresh rosemary or thyme

salt and pepper

||||||||||||||||||||||||||||||||||||||||||||||||||||||||||||||||||||||||||||||||||||||||||||

1   Preheat the kamado to 250°F.

2   Trim the roast. Using a sharp boning knife, remove the "lip," which is a 1- to 2-inch piece of hard, white fat along one side of the roast. Then remove the fat cap by working your fingers under the tough membrane and lifting it up towards the other edge. Use the boning knife to free up any stubborn parts where it doesn't want to separate from the roast. When you have the cap peeled back to where it joins the other side, remove the membrane completely with the boning knife.

3   Tie the roast. Use kitchen twine and tie the roast every 1 to 2 inches. This isn't just for looks; it will help the roast cook evenly. If you don't know how to tie a roast, you can either look up a video tutorial or just cheat and tightly tie 1 piece of kitchen twine around the roast every 1 to 2 inches.

4   Season the roast. Mix a slather by whisking the water, beef base, and Worcestershire sauce together in a small bowl. Using your hands, rub the mixture over all sides of the roast. Next, season with the rub, 3 tablespoons of NMT Beef Rub is enough to do a whole 13- to 15-pound prime rib. If yours is smaller, just use enough to cover the roast. Season it heavier than you think you will need as you are only seasoning the exterior of a large roast.

5   Place the beef stock, garlic, and rosemary or thyme into the roasting pan. Top with a rack and the roast. Insert the probe from a remote thermometer into the center of the roast.

6   Place the roasting pan, rack, and roast onto the grill and close the lid. Cook for 90 minutes and then flip the roast over. Continue cooking until the roast reaches an internal temperature of 127°F. Wearing your protective gloves, remove the roasting pan, rack, and roast. Set aside while waiting for the grill temperature to rise.

7   Open the bottom and top vents to raise the cooking temperature to 550°F.

Once the internal temperature of the roast begins to fall, return it to the grill and sear for 1 minute on each side.

8   Remove to a resting rack and allow to cool.

9   Strain the au jus and use a fat separator to skim off the fat. In a saucepan over medium-low heat, bring the au jus to a simmer. Taste for seasoning and add salt, pepper, and/or water to taste as needed.

Slice the roast and serve with the au jus.

APPENDIX: TROUBLESHOOTING

These are just some first steps that you can take in order to troubleshoot problems that you may encounter with cooking on your kamado. Each problem can be affected by many factors, too many to consider here. If you're still having problems, I have an online companion page on Nibble Me This where I have the most up-to-date information and you can reach me with further questions.

FIRE MANAGEMENT

KAMADO CAN'T REACH HIGHER TEMPERATURES

- **Blocked air vents** — Clean out your kamado and make sure that the holes in your fire bowl and fire grate are free of ash, coals, or other debris that will block airflow.

- **Vent slot misaligned** — The opening at the bottom of your fire bowl should line up with the hole for the lower vent. If it is turned away from that hole, the airflow is impeded.

- **Thermometer calibration** — It could be a false reading on your thermometer. Calibrate your thermometer to check for accuracy.

KAMADO WON'T HOLD LOWER TEMPERATURES / KAMADO GETS TOO HOT

- **Too hot too soon** — Getting a kamado to come down in temperature after it has already gotten too hot can be difficult. Keep a close eye on your temperatures while preheating and slowly come up to your desired cooking temperature. I start shutting the lower vent in increments once I am 50°F–75°F less than my target temperature so I can coast up into it.

- **Lighting all of the coal at once** — The kamado isn't best suited for dumping in a chimney of hot coals like other grills. Review the sections on lighting a kamado (page 5).

- **Air leaks** — If your kamado has air leaks and is allowing air to enter at places other than the two vents, you don't have total control of airflow and temperatures.

  Gaskets — Watch for smoke coming through your gaskets while smoking. If your kamado is properly aligned but is leaking smoke here, you should consider replacing your gaskets.

  Lower vent — Visually inspect your lower vent and draft door for air leaks. With a brand new kamado we found that it was leaking between the ceramic base and vent. We removed the vent, sealed the back, top, and bottom of it with a high-temp caulk and then put the vent back on. We also found that in certain positions, the draft door also had a gap. We put shims between the door and door track, which pushed the door into place.

  Alignment — If the dome lid and base aren't lined up correctly, you may have air gaps around the gasket that has nothing to do with the gasket being faulty. Do the "dollar bill test" by placing a dollar on the gasket, shutting the dome lid, and then pulling on the dollar bill. You should experience slight resistance. Repeat this around the rim looking for gaps. Consult your manufacturer for specific realignment instructions as these vary from kamado to kamado.

FIRE WENT OUT DURING OVERNIGHT COOK

- **Temperature not stabilized** — Make sure the fire is completely stable at your desired temperature before throwing in all of your food and walking away. For overnight cooks, I like to see my empty kamado hold the cooking temperature for at least 15 minutes before loading it with food.

- **Coals blocking air vents** — Use a wiggle rod (metal skewer or coat hanger with one inch of the end bent at a 90° angle) during the cook, especially after several hours of cooking. Enter through the bottom vent and clear the fire grate holes of any coal or ash.

NOT ENOUGH SMOKE

The efficient design of the kamado also means that it doesn't burn as much fuel and doesn't create as much smoke.

- **Not enough wood** — Add more chunks, chips, or splits of wood and make sure that it is mixed throughout your coal, from the top to the bottom and on all sides.

- **Meat too warm** — For smoking, keep your meat cold until it goes on the smoker. Cold meat will be on the smoker longer, absorbing more smoke. Smoke ring formation happens mostly when the meat is below 140°F but the meat will continue to develop smoke flavor above that temperature.

TOO MUCH SMOKE

- Incomplete combustion — Typically this is caused by putting the food on too early before the fire has changed from a dense white smoke to a thin "blue" or almost clear smoke. A dirty burning fire will deposit soot, creosote, and other bad flavors on your meat. Make sure your fire is burning cleanly before adding your meats.

MAINTENANCE

INACCURATE THERMOMETER

- Remove your thermometer and carefully lower its probe (not the entire thing) into a pot of rapidly boiling water to get a

temperature reading. Use a wrench to secure the calibration nut on the back of the thermometer and turn until the thermometer reads 212°F (or calculate the boiling point for your altitude). Note: some thermometers aren't designed to be calibrated and some cheap models won't hold calibration for long. These should just be replaced.

BROKEN PLATE SETTER

- Have broken legs on two plate setters by knocking them over or dropping them? I repaired them using J-B Weld (found at automotive stores) and they have lasted that way for over five years.

KAMADO IS FROZEN SHUT

- **Truly frozen from moisture and cold temps** — Open the lower and top vents. Light a starter cube and either drop it down into the coals from the top vent (if there is nothing blocking the coals below) or slide it in through the bottom vent. This will warm up your grill and melt the ice.

- **Gasket adhesive** — If your gasket is torched and the top and bottom are fused together, you can try to work around the edges and carefully pry it open with something like a putty knife. Worst case scenario, you can just rip off and replace the gasket.

BLOWN GASKET

- The gaskets will wear out especially with a lot of high-temperature cooks, misaligned domes, or cooking with the lid open. You can cook on a kamado without a gasket as long as there is a tight connection between the lid and base. I cooked on a kamado without a gasket for three to four years without a problem. Some manufacturers offer a higher-temperature-rated gasket made out of Nomex. My personal favorite is using a gasket intended for wood stoves as a replacement; however, these aren't "approved" or rated for cooking equipment.

COMMON CONVERSIONS

1 gallon = 4 quarts = 8 pints = 16 cups = 128 fluid ounces = 3.8 liters

1 quart = 2 pints = 4 cups = 32 ounces = .95 liter

1 pint = 2 cups = 16 ounces = 480 ml

1 cup = 8 ounces = 240 ml

¼ cup = 4 tablespoons = 12 teaspoons = 2 ounces = 60 ml

TEMPERATURE CONVERSIONS

Fahrenheit (°F)	Celsius (°C)
200°F	95°C
225°F	110°C
250°F	120°C
275°F	135°C
300°F	150°C
325°F	165°C
350°F	175°C
375°F	190°C
400°F	200°C
425°F	220°C
450°F	230°C
475°F	245°C

Volume Conversions

U.S.	U.S. equivalent	Metric
1 tablespoon (3 teaspoons)	½ fluid ounce	15 milliliters
¼ cup	2 fluid ounces	60 milliliters
⅓ cup	3 fluid ounces	90 milliliters
½ cup	4 fluid ounces	120 milliliters
⅔ cup	5 fluid ounces	150 milliliters
¾ cup	6 fluid ounces	180 milliliters
1 cup	8 fluid ounces	240 milliliters
2 cups	16 fluid ounces	480 milliliters

Weight Conversions

U.S.	Metric
½ ounce	15 grams
1 ounce	30 grams
2 ounces	60 grams
¼ pound	115 grams
⅓ pound	150 grams
½ pound	225 grams
¾ pound	350 grams
1 pound	450 grams

INDEX

ACKNOWLEDGMENTS

I'd like to thank my family for putting up with this barbecue passion of mine, which started off as a hobby and ended up being an obsession. Special thanks to my wife, Alexis—for making numerous trips to the grocery store when I'd forgotten a key ingredient, for tolerating the hoard of grills at our house, and for taking over the food styling for me.

Thanks also go out to some of the best people on Earth, my barbecue family. Thanks to:

- My neighbors and fellow Eggheads, John and Anna Mae, for being my sounding board for my blog and this book.

- Meathead of AmazingRibs.com (best BBQ site on the web!) for prodding me to take on this challenge.

- Chris Lilly, Ken Hess, and the Big Bob Gibson's Barbecue crew for so much help over the last few years and for giving me the confidence to write this book.

- All of the great people on the BBQ Brethren, Big Green Egg, and Kamado Guru forums.

- My sponsors, including Craycort Cast Iron Grates, Kingsford, Johnsonville, Char-Broil, Thermoworks, Meyer Natural Beef, and the National Pork Board for their support and especially the hands-on learning opportunities.

There are others too numerous to name but all have unfailingly shared knowledge, ideas, and support along the way.

ABOUT THE AUTHOR

Chris Grove is the publisher and resident pitmaster of the popular grilling and barbecue blog Nibble Me This (www .nibblemethis.com).

Chris fell in love with all things barbecue when he was seven years old and had his first taste of true smoked pork on his grandparents' farm in North Carolina. That vinegary Carolina chopped pork started a fire that burns in him to this day, driving him to be a "perpetual BBQ student." He seeks out every opportunity to learn from the masters and takes every chance he can get to find out more about grilling and barbecue—the day he thinks he knows it all will be the day it's time to quit.

Chris and his wife are Certified BBQ Judges with the Kansas City Barbecue Society and enjoy traveling to attend, judge, or compete in barbecue contests and events across the South. He sees the competition as a way to sharpen his game as well as to study what others are doing to improve their 'que.

In addition to Nibble Me This, Chris's recipes and photographs have been featured in national media outlets. He works with companies in the grilling, BBQ, and food industries to stay on top of new trends and gather the latest information. Whether it's traveling to cattle ranches in Montana or pig farms in Ohio, he's out learning what goes into making the best food on the grill.

While all of this has been fun, Chris's true passion is experimenting with his grills and developing recipes for the backyard chef.

He can be found on www.nibblemethis.com, on Twitter (@nibblemethis), or on Facebook (www.facebook.com/NibbleMeThis2).

Looking for More Great Cookbooks?
We would like to suggest:

Exclusively Kamado
50 Innovative Recipes for Your
Ceramic Smoker and Grill

by Paul Sidoriak

The Simple Art of
Salt Block Cooking
Grill, Cure, Bake and Serve with
Himalayan Salt Blocks

by Jessica Harlan and Kelley Sparwasser

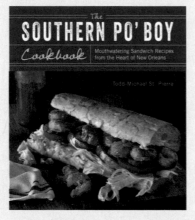

The Southern Po' Boy Cookbook
Mouthwatering Sandwich Recipes
from the Heart of New Orleans

by Todd-Michael St. Pierre

Homemade Condiments
Artisan Recipes Using Fresh,
Natural Ingredients

by Jessica Harlan

Get more info at: www.ulyssespress.com/cooking